IMAGES
of America

CENTRAL OHIO'S
HISTORIC PRISONS

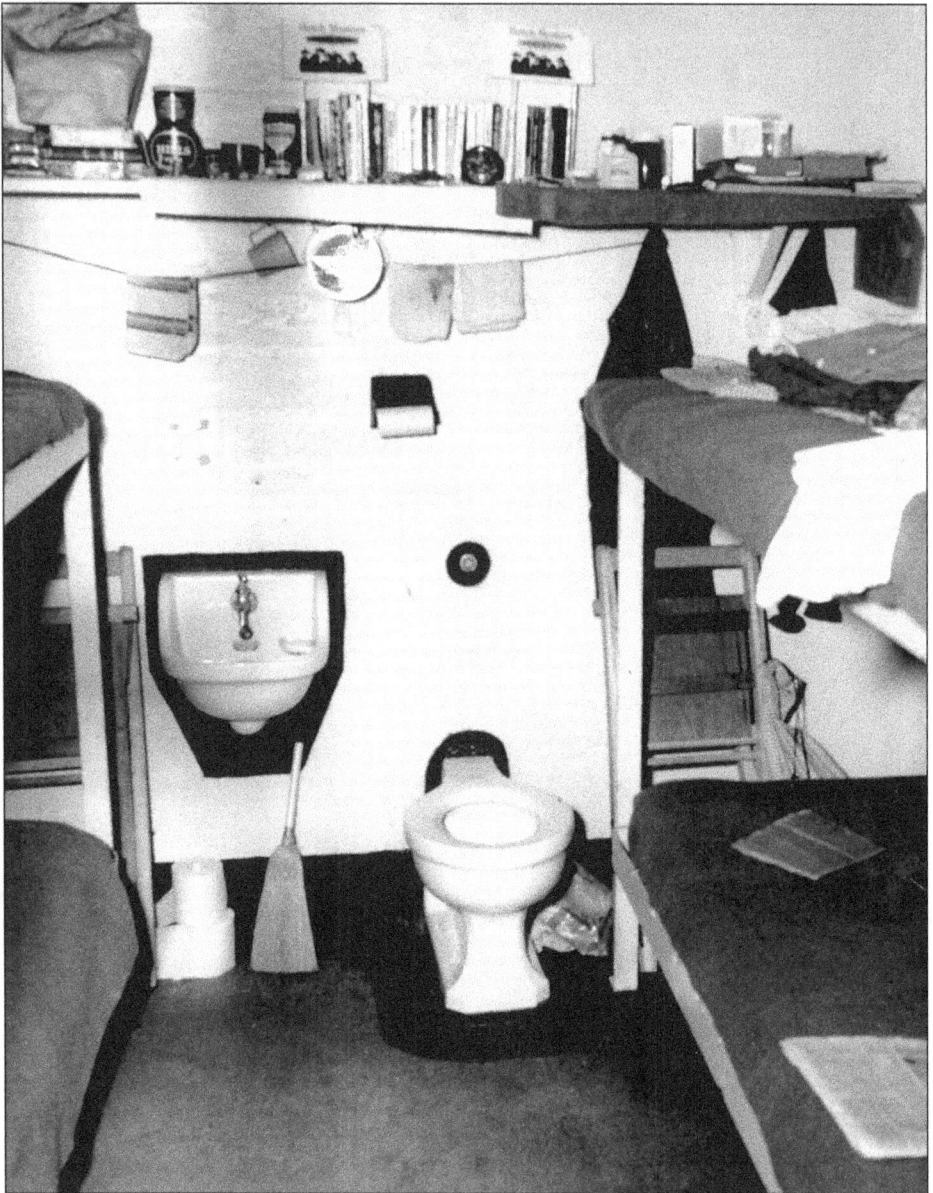

In 2004, *Forbes* published an article on "Best Places To Go To Prison." Although the Ohio Penitentiary had been closed 20 years by then, there was little chance it would have made the list, anyway. As this photograph of a four-man cell illustrates, no one would have mistaken the antiquated facility for a country club. The inmates lived in a space about the size of a backyard garden shed. (CCCJ.)

On the cover: "East Block" at the Ohio State Reformatory in Mansfield is believed to be the largest, freestanding, all-steel cellblock in the world (although there are rumors of a larger one in Russia). It is six tiers high with two ranges (sides) per tier and 50 cells per range, for a total of 600 two-man cells and a designed capacity of 1,200. A central maintenance shaft separates the ranges. (Courtesy of Columbus Citizen and Citizen Journal Collection/Scripps-Howard Newspapers, Grandview Heights Public Library/Photohio.org.)

IMAGES
of America

CENTRAL OHIO'S HISTORIC PRISONS

David Meyers and Elise Meyers

ARCADIA
PUBLISHING

Published by Arcadia Publishing
Charleston, South Carolina

Library of Congress Control Number: 2009921939

For all general information contact Arcadia Publishing at:
Telephone 843-853-2070
Fax 843-853-0044
E-mail sales@arcadiapublishing.com
For customer service and orders:
Toll-Free 1-888-313-2665

Visit us on the Internet at www.arcadiapublishing.com

Some of the finest people I have known were working in some of the most thankless jobs imaginable. This book is dedicated to them.

CONTENTS

ACKNOWLEDGMENTS

This book would have been impossible without the support of Rebecca Felkner and Wes Osborn, who allowed us use of the Grandview Heights Public Library's Columbus Citizen and Citizen-Journal Collection (CCCJ). The official attribution is, Columbus Citizen and Citizen Journal Collection/Scripps-Howard Newspapers, Grandview Heights Public Library/Photohio.org.

We are also indebted to the BIS/FSB Historical Museum (BIS/FSB), Inc., particularly Mike Tharp and Cindy Hillis, for their photographs, memories, and friendship.

Lee Tasseff of the Mansfield/Richland County Convention and Visitors Bureau (MRCCVB) and Dan Seckel of the Mansfield Reformatory Preservation Society (www.mrps.org) were also of assistance. And a "tip of the Hatlo hat" to Ted Glattke (TG), Dave Randall (DR), Larry Moore, Warren Francis (WF), Randy McNutt (RM), Sam Walker, and, especially, Beverly Meyers for their encouragement.

Finally we would like to thank Julie Callahan and Nick Taggart of the Columbus Metropolitan Library (CML) for their help in obtaining images from the library's collection.

The photograph of Chester Himes is from the Library of Congress (LOC), Prints and Photographs Division, Carl Van Vechten Collection, (reproduction number, LC-USZ62-105578 DLC). The Manfred Marsden Griswold photographs are from the National Archives (NA).

All other images are from the authors' personal collection.

INTRODUCTION

On April 7, 1788, the Ohio Company named their new settlement on the banks of the Ohio River "Marietta" in honor of Marie Antoinette, Queen of France. Within four years, the citizens of Marietta, mostly members of prominent New England families, were making plans to build a courthouse—and a jail. By 1793, however, the need for the latter had become so pressing that an "old log house" was adapted for that purpose.

Although it would be 10 more years before Ohio achieved statehood, its first English speaking community already had a jail of sorts. (Meanwhile, the recently widowed queen was, herself, locked away as prisoner No. 280 in the Conciergerie, a former royal palace in Paris, while awaiting a date with the guillotine.)

Historically a jail or prison was a place to confine individuals accused of crimes before they went to trial. Under the British system, those found guilty were subjected to some manner of corporal or capital punishment—generally, flogging, bodily mutilation, or hanging. The idea of sentencing someone to a period of imprisonment was unknown except for debtors, derelicts, and vagrants, who were placed in a workhouse to perform hard labor.

By the time the Ohio Company arrived in the Northwest Territory, Americans were beginning to question the value of punishing criminal offenders. On September 6, 1788, Gov. Arthur St. Clair and three judges passed the first legislation in the territory regarding crimes and criminals. Of the 20 offenses and their specified penalties, murder was the only one punishable by death, possibly the first criminal code in the world to impose such a limitation.

Two years later, the first penitentiary in the United States was established at Philadelphia's Walnut Street Gaol. It consisted of a central corridor with cells lining either side. The intent was to discourage crime by segregating prisoners through solitary confinement. The word "penitentiary" originated with Pennsylvania's Quakers, who believed that penitence and self-examination would lead the prisoners to salvation.

Over the next 40 years, two distinct prison models emerged. In 1817, the Auburn Plan of industry, obedience, and silence, was established in New York's Auburn State Prison. While working together during the day, prisoners observed a strict code of silence, and then at night they were housed in individual cells. In 1829, Pennsylvania's Eastern State Penitentiary instituted the Pennsylvania System, which employed solitary confinement both day and night. The Auburn Plan eventually won out primarily for economic reasons (although it was also observed that the Pennsylvania System tended to promote mental illness).

In his annual message to the Ohio State Legislature on December 3, 1811, Gov. Return Jonathan Meigs discussed the need to build a state prison. In response, a group calling themselves the Proprietors of Columbus offered to donate two 10-acre plots of land, one for a prison and the other for a state house, along with $50,000 in cash.

The legislature accepted the offer on February 14, 1912, and construction of the first penitentiary in Ohio began the following year. Completed in 1815, it was also the first public building erected in the capital city. The prison was variously called the state penitentiary or the state prison, but in 1822 it was officially named the Ohio Penitentiary.

Not surprisingly, the Ohio Penitentiary soon proved to be of insufficient size to accommodate the needs of the courts. By 1826, Gov. Jeremiah Morrow was calling for the construction of "more capacious prisons," but no funding was provided. The following year, Gov. Allen Trimble advocated either enlarging the existing prison or erecting a new one "on a more improved plan."

Still no action was taken until 1833, when work began on a new prison. The original prison did not reflect any particular model, but the new one followed the Auburn Plan. A visitor to the city a couple of years later described the Ohio Penitentiary as "truly a noble structure, an ornament to the city and an honor to the state, and when completed will probably be second to none in the country." While the facility remained in use until 1984, it had long ceased to be "an honor" to the state.

On April 16, 1857, at the urging of Gov. Salmon P. Chase, the Ohio General Assembly established the Ohio State Farm as a penal institution for boys between the ages of 8 and 18—boys who until then had been confined in the Ohio Penitentiary along with adult inmates. Cincinnati's Charles Reemelin was appointed one of three commissioners of the institution.

A native of Germany, Reemelin's first act was to visit many of the existing institutions for youthful offenders in the United States. However, when he found they were all "of the walled-in class," he traveled to England, France, and Germany at his own expense (although he had hoped to be reimbursed) to inspect their facilities.

Particularly impressed by France's Colonie de Mettray, Reemelin returned to Ohio determined to model the Ohio Reform Farm and School, as it came to be called, on the "family" or "cottage" system. It was constructed on 1,210 acres in the Hocking Hills, approximately six miles south of Lancaster in Fairfield County. The institution was renamed the Boys' Industrial School in 1884, and was known as the Fairfield School for Boys when it closed in 1980.

As early as 1868, the Board of State Charities had argued for the establishment of a new prison, an intermediate penitentiary designed exclusively to accommodate young men. Allen O. Myers, chairman of the committee of prisons and prison reform (and a "graduate" of the Ohio Reform School as a youth), enlisted the support of Gov. George Hoadly in advocating the creation of a "grand system of graded prisons; with the reform farm on one side of the new prison, for juvenile offenders, and the penitentiary on the other, for all the more hardened and incorrigible class."

However, these recommendations went unheeded until the 66th General Assembly of 1884–1885 enacted a series of laws codifying the primary ideas of the New York's Elmira State Reformatory system. Camp Mordecai Bartley, a former Civil War training facility near Mansfield, was offered as the site for the new prison. Even though the cornerstone was laid in November 1886, construction was not sufficiently advanced until September 1896 to allow 150 short-term inmates to be transferred from the Ohio Penitentiary. The Ohio State Reformatory, as it was called, remained in operation for 94 years.

As celebrated social reformer F. B. Sanborn of Massachusetts declared in 1887 at the National Conference of Charities and Corrections, "In Ohio, the board [of State Charities] has succeeded in establishing the most complete prison system, in theory, which exists in the United States. And this system is advancing toward practical development."

In *Central Ohio's Historic Prisons*, we take a detailed look at the three 19th century Ohio prisons that laid the foundation for the state's correctional system and, taken together, established a model that was replicated by others. Each of these institutions was once viewed as the best the country had to offer and, yet, each was later condemned, justifiably, when it fell behind the times. Unfortunately it is a pattern the state has had difficulty breaking.

—David Meyers

One

OHIO PENITENTIARY LIGHTS AND SHADOWS

In 1804, the Franklin County Court of Common Pleas ordered the construction of the first jail in what would soon become the state capital, Columbus. Located in Franklinton, not far from the Scioto River, the jail consisted of a collection of log buildings with 13 whipping posts encircled by a stockade fence.

As Dan Morgan wrote in *Lights and Shadows of the Ohio Penitentiary*, "Not only men but women and children were brought there, stripped of their clothing, lashed to the cruel posts and whipped until their backs resembled 'raw beef,' then tied face downward on the cold ground while shovels of hot ashes and coals of fire were sprinkled on the raw and bleeding flesh."

This was what passed for justice 28 years after the United States became a country and just one year after Ohio became a state.

The first state prison, also built in Columbus, was the Ohio Penitentiary, consisting of 13 cells: 9 "light" (windowed) and 4 "dark." With the completion of the prison in 1815, and the passage of a statute providing for the punishment of crime by imprisonment in the penitentiary, a new age in corrections had begun.

As a result, offenses that once earned the offender a whipping could now result in his imprisonment. The first inmates, brothers John and David Evans, ages 19 and 20 respectively, arrived at the prison on August 18, 1815, having been convicted of assault and battery with intent to murder and rob.

The rated capacity of the facility was 60 men, including the dark cells. However, by the following year, it was projected that they would need to house at least 110 within three and a half years. Over the next century and a half, this number would continue to increase dramatically until it peaked at 5,235 in April 1955.

The first keeper, James Kooken, hired Col. Griffith Thomas as his clerk and three or four guards. The keeper's duty was "to contract and purchase tools and clothing for the prisoners, to keep separate accounts relating to the maintenance of the prisoners, to the articles manufactured and sold, and to materials and stock on hands; to provide coarse and wholesome food for the prisoners, to punish convicts by confinement in solitary cells, and to pay all prison debts."

The job of keeper or warden quickly became a political "spoil," much to its detriment.

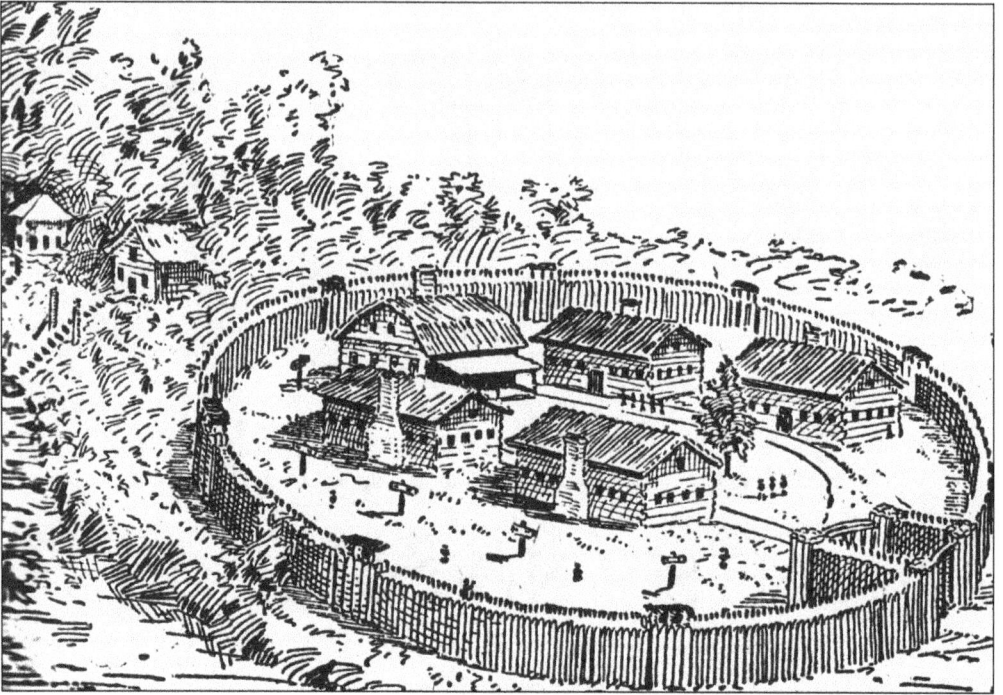

In 1803, having attained the required population of 60,000, Ohio was the first of five states carved out of the Northwest Territory. The following year, the first jail was ordered built in what would eventually become Columbus. Although this sketch may have been drawn from imagination rather than memory, it is correct in the essentials. The jail was a crude affair resembling a pioneer outpost. (Authors' collection.)

Completed in 1815, the first Ohio Penitentiary was a brick building on a stone foundation located at Friend (now Main) and Scioto Streets. Three stories high, including the basement, it was 30 feet wide and 60 feet long. It abutted a prison yard 100 feet by 160 feet, enclosed by a wall 15 feet high. The top floor and the basement could only be entered from the yard. (Authors' collection.)

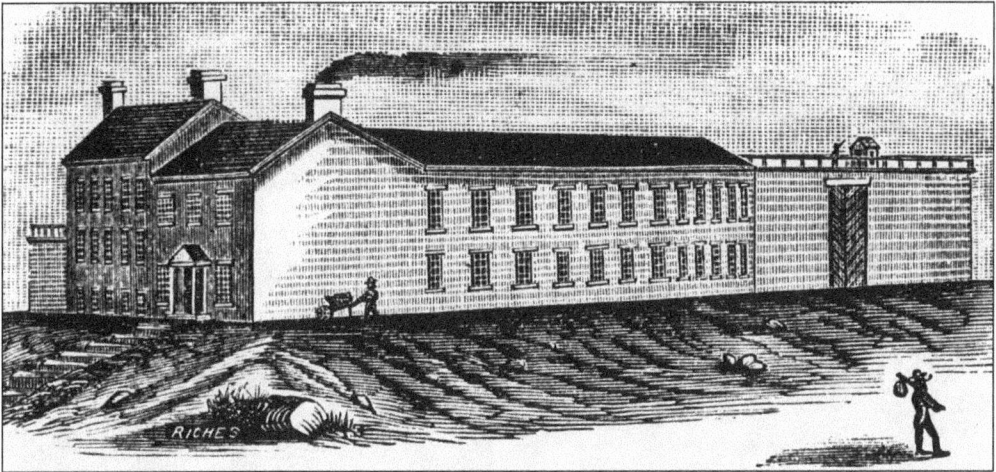

Only three years later, a new prison was built nearby. A two-story brick building on a stone foundation, it was 50 feet long by 36 feet wide. It contained 54 aboveground cells and 5 belowground (entered by a trap-door). The outside wall was 400 feet by 160 feet, with a plank walk with a handrail on top. The former prison became the keeper's residence. (Authors' collection.)

By 1820, the existing prison was also deemed too small by the standing committee on the penitentiary. Still work did not begin on a replacement until 1833. Then on October 28–29, 1934, the inmates were marched from the old penitentiary to the new one on Spring Street. Construction was not completed until 1837. In 1997, 160 years later, it was razed to make way for the Arena District development. (Authors' collection.)

This woodblock print from 1840 shows the Ohio Penitentiary from inside the prison yard looking south toward the cellblock. On either side are the industrial buildings where prisoners were put to work manufacturing harnesses, shoes, barrels, brooms, silk hats, bolts, tailored goods, and other items not otherwise manufactured in Ohio. The inmates were forced to march in lockstep whenever they moved within the prison. (Authors' collection.)

Early prison managers believed in hard work, harsh discipline, and large doses of religion. Consequently, as this 1852 print shows, the inmates were expected to attend weekly religious services. In truth, church services offered the prisoners a brief respite from their otherwise bleak existence. As early as 1835, Rev. Russell Bigelow had been appointed chaplain, but funding for the position was eliminated two years later. (Authors' collection.)

As he records in *Memorials of Prison Life*, Methodist preacher James B. Finley became chaplain of the Ohio Penitentiary in 1846, where he remained for three years before resigning due to poor health. A drunken ruffian as a youth, he was known as the "New Market Devil" before he found religion and became a social reformer, speaking out against slavery, the evils of alcohol, and inhumane prison conditions. (Authors' collection.)

Finley's initial impressions were that, "Here were all ranks and ages, from the man of high life to the meanest pickpocket, from the gray-haired man of eighty down to the boy of fourteen years. They were all dressed in striped clothing; all seemed depressed and broken down in spirits; all were silently at work, without the hope of remuneration, under the inspection of well-appointed watchers." (Authors' collection.)

An inmate serving a 15-year sentence for counterfeiting drew this 1875 bird's-eye view of the Ohio Penitentiary. Throughout its history, the prison was constrained by the 30-foot stone wall which encircled it. However, numerous changes took place as buildings were added, replaced, remodeled, and repurposed. Ironically a 60-foot section of the wall collapsed without warning on July 6, 1994, 10 years after the prison closed. (Authors' collection.)

Between 1834 and 1877, the prison expanded several times. East Hall was completed in 1861, adding 500 more cells to West Hall's original 200. New Hall, which paralleled Neil (formerly Dennison) Avenue, was completed in 1877. These three halls formed an impressive 813-foot facade overlooking Spring Street. Many of the shop buildings had to be rebuilt over the years due to periodic fires set by disgruntled prisoners. (CML.)

14

BANKERS ROW, OHIO STATE PENITENTIARY,
COLUMBUS, OHIO.

The Ohio Penitentiary maintained a block of cells that was outfitted for "privileged convicts" (what are now called "white collar" criminals). Dubbed "Bankers' Row," each of the cells had a carpet on the floor, a curtain covering the door, and a mirror, among other furnishings. The denizens of Bankers' Row wore white shirts, generally held clerk positions in the prison, and were permitted to purchase their own food. (CML.)

Although prisoners complained about a diet of corn, molasses, and bread, they still ate better than many who lived outside the prison walls. As this 1899 photograph shows, the poor people of Columbus once lined up outside the prison gates to wait for the inmates to finish eating so they could have the scraps. They brought containers with them to carry away what was ever leftover. (Authors' collection.)

At the dawn of the 20th century, the warden and his family lived in relative luxury, waited on hand and foot by inmate trustees who performed all the domestic chores. Some of the wardens and their officers were clearly corrupt and used their positions to enrich themselves. The contract labor system enabled them to personally profit from the toil of the inmates who were paid a pittance for their work. (Authors' collection.)

On December 26, 1896, guard S. J. Temple shot two prisoners, killing one, in the Reynolds Foundry, after they had struck him on the head with an iron bar. Inmates had virtually taken control of the foundry (the most despised work assignment) during the previous week and warned Temple not to try to enforce the rules. Tipped off about a plot to kill him, Temple brought a pistol to work. (Authors' collection.)

Originally built in 1895, the James Hospital was "modernized" in 1944 and renovated again in 1968 after it was heavily damaged by fire. To the prisoners, it was the "St. James Infirmary" memorialized in the famous blues song. Although provision was made for hiring a physician as early as 1821, the role was actually fulfilled by an inmate who happened to be a doctor. (CCCJ.)

During the 1968 riots, the penitentiary auditorium was heavily damaged by fire and smoke. Over the years, many celebrities had appeared on its stage, from fighters Joe Lewis and Jack Dempsey to musician Lionel Hampton and various local college and church groups. James Thurber's Scarlet Mask production, "Oh My, Omar," was staged there for the benefit of the inmates, although Thurber was too drunk to attend. (CCCJ.)

Not all prisoners lived in cells. Some were housed in large dormitories with dozens of other inmates. A feature of the dormitories at the Ohio Penitentiary was a pool table. However, instead of pool balls, the inmates played with wooden disks that slid across the table on a bed of sawdust. Some inmates became as accomplished at this unorthodox game as any pool shark. (CCCJ.)

A prison kitchen is like any other kitchen except it has been constructed on a Brobdingnagian scale with massive gas ranges, steam kettles, tilt skillets, steam cabinets, deep fryers, and the like, in addition to the regular appliances. Since inmate food service workers have access to all manner of cutlery, tool control is extremely important, lest someone smuggle a knife or other dangerous implement out into the general population. (CCCJ.)

A well-run mess hall is imperative in any penal institution. The time devoted to feeding the inmate population determines what the institutional schedule will look like. Prisoners cannot be sent off to work or school until they have been fed. If the mess hall is not sufficiently large or efficient, there will be little time available for other programming. Consequently inmates may not linger over their meals. (CCCJ.)

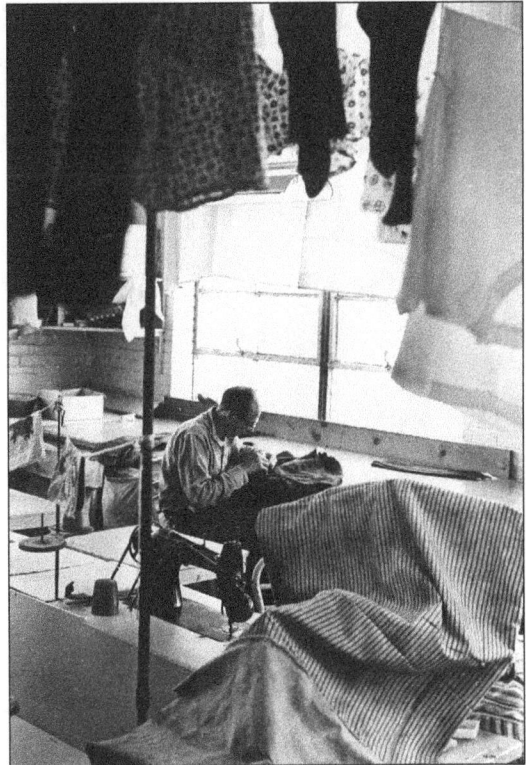

Inmates who worked in the tailor shop generally took more care when making their own clothes. Whereas the other prisoners had to take the shirts, trousers, and jacket issued to them by the quartermaster, the inmate tailor made sure his personal clothing fit his exact measurements. A few of them also secretly made items of civilian clothing to wear in an escape attempt. (CCCJ.)

In 1895, the Wolfe brothers from Corning, Ohio, established the Wolfe Brothers Shoe Company in Columbus, before going on to purchase the *Ohio State Journal* and the *Columbus Dispatch*. Corning historian Jeff Ferguson was told one of them learned shoemaking while doing time at the Ohio Penitentiary. However, it seems more likely the brother would have learned the trade from his father, Andrew, a lifelong shoemaker. (CCCJ.)

The gang shower at the Ohio Penitentiary was no place for the faint of heart. Nicknamed "The Car Wash," the shower was where the prisoners were the most vulnerable. Many scores were settled here when a prisoner would "accidentally slip on a bar of soap" and take a "fall." A fortunate few had work assignments in departments that had their own, more private, shower facilities. (CCCJ.)

Inmates who were brought before the Ohio Penitentiary Rules Infraction Board, the institutional court, risked being sent to a correctional cell (or "the hole") if their behavior warranted it. The purpose of such a sentence was to isolate the prisoner from the rest of the institution to the greatest extent possible. Occasionally an inmate would seek to be placed in isolation just to get away from other inmates. (CCCJ.)

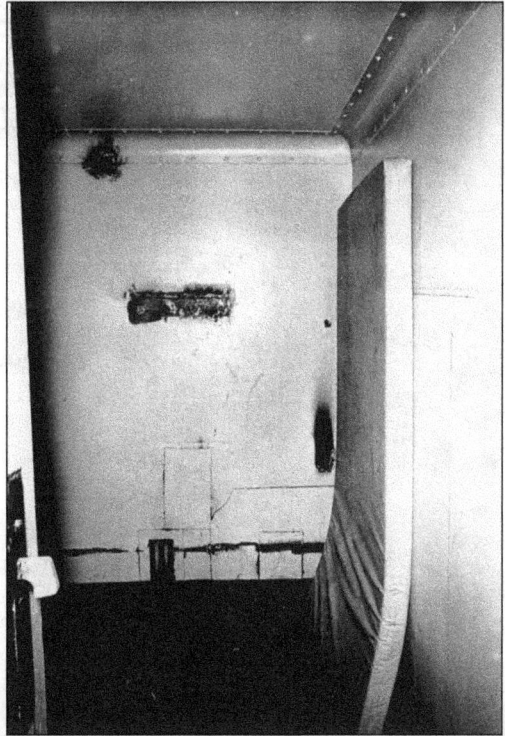

There were two deputy wardens in the penitentiary: one for custody and the other for treatment. The Psychology Department occupied the second floor of the so-called Treatment Services Building. Every inmate admitted to the institution was administered a battery of psychological and educational assessments, including the Ohio Penal Classification Test, which was designed specifically to assess the mental abilities of a prison population. (CCCJ.)

In 1960, the Ohio Penitentiary occupied 23.34 acres and included the following buildings: administration (1), honor dormitory (2), academic school (3), Catholic chapel (4), treatment services (5), James Hospital (6), dormitories and warehousing (7), dining rooms and kitchen (8), vocational school and laundry (9), power plant (10), penal industry (11), woolen mill (12), cotton mill (13), dormitories (14), Protestant chapel and auditorium (15), cellblocks (16), and dormitories and gymnasium (17). Many of them were old and dilapidated owing to years of abuse and neglect. In April 1913, the general assembly had established the London Prison Farm, 27 miles southwest of Columbus, as a branch of the Ohio Penitentiary, with the idea "to save men," in the words of Gov. James M. Cox: "Money is not our object, the State of Ohio does not want to coin gold out of the tears of unfortunates." It was spun off as a separate prison in 1924. (CCCJ.)

Two

BOREDOM AND TERROR BEHIND THE WALLS

Inmates are fond of saying, "Do the time; don't let the time do you." What they mean is this: to survive in prison, one has to accept the situation, keep busy, and forget about anything beyond the walls. Those who fail to do so will only drive themselves crazy and wind up in "the psych ward" (or, in earlier days, the separate "Insane Asylum" housed within the prison). For the most part, "doing time" is learning to cope with months of boredom and, occasionally, moments of terror.

Generally speaking, inmates prefer a controlled, predictable environment because their foremost concern is their own safety. They do not have much tolerance for the younger, immature, and hyperactive inmates stirring things up in their "house." Most of the time, they allow the guards or correctional officers to have enough power to maintain order, but it would be foolhardy to think they cannot take it back whenever they like.

During its history, the Ohio Penitentiary was witness to some truly harrowing events. Without a doubt, the darkest day in the prison's history was the Easter Monday fire of April 21, 1930, in which 322 inmates perished. It was front-page news across the country, and within 21 hours, New York moviegoers were watching Pathé Newsreel footage of the disaster. Just three days later, Charlotte and Bob Miller released the first of four recordings of the mawkish ballad, "Ohio Prison Fire."

Two major riots also took place at the Ohio Penitentiary. The first was the so-called Halloween Riot that occurred on October 31, 1952. In retrospect, this incident proved to be a good training exercise for the law enforcement agencies that would have to contend with the even more serious riot of August 20, 1968. Some 25 years later, on April 11, 1993, the deadliest riot of all took place at the Southern Ohio Correctional Facility in Lucasville, which had been built to replace the Ohio Penitentiary.

In many instances, the moments of terror arise out of the months of boredom. "Idle hands are the devil's workshop," as the old saying goes. During periods of overcrowding, the ability to keep inmates busy is often an insurmountable challenge because there simply is not enough room in the work and education programs. An idle inmate discovers that "the time is doing him" and lashes out in frustration. A riot is always a good attention-getter.

In a ranking of the deadliest fires in American history, the Ohio Penitentiary Fire comes in at number seven, just ahead of the great Chicago fire of 1871 (in which 300 lives were lost) and just behind the Hoboken Docks Fire of 1900 (in which 326 died). The total number of deaths at the Ohio Penitentiary was 322, making it the worst prison fire ever. (CCCJ.)

It was about 5:30 p.m. on April 21, 1930, the day after Easter. As investigators later determined, a candle left on the roof of the West Hall apparently ignited some oily rags. Three inmates were accused of having deliberately started the fire as a diversion while they made an escape attempt. Two of the accused later committed suicide. This is looking north into cellblock I-K. (CCCJ.)

Critics of warden Preston Thomas claimed the prisoners were scapegoated to divert attention from his administration's poor handling of the crisis. A clear breakdown of command structure had occurred; armed militia (shown) had to be brought in to establish control, and Attorney General Gilbert Bettman's report suggested the likely cause of the fire was an exposed light bulb breaking against a piece of steel in a construction area. (CCCJ.)

Having already been locked in their cells for the night, many inmates were trapped in "a giant bird cage," as Gov. Myers Y. Cooper later said. While some died from direct exposure to the intense flames, others succumbed to smoke inhalation, especially those on the upper two tiers. At the time, there were three times as many prisoners in the penitentiary as it was designed to hold. (Authors' collection.)

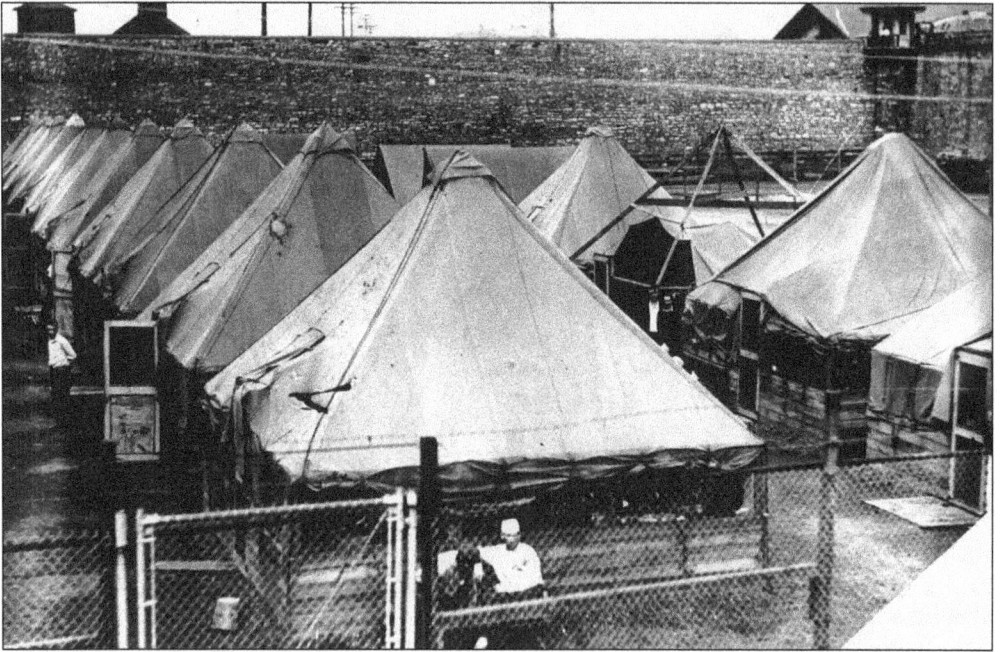

After the fire, inmates in "White City" (so-called because the cellblock was painted white) went on a rampage for nine days, destroying locks and ripping off cell doors. When they were finally subdued by troops, they were housed in tents set up in the prison yard. As early as 1908, concerns had been raised about the overcrowded conditions. Several hundred surviving inmates were transferred to the London Prison Farm. (CCCJ.)

The prison did not have adequate firefighting equipment, but firefighters from the city of Columbus responded within 15 minutes to find prisoners freely roaming the yard. Warden Preston Thomas later admitted he did not have a plan for how to deal with fires, but relied upon "common sense." After Thomas was removed from office, Gov. Myers Y. Cooper received a petition asking that he be reinstated. (CCCJ.)

A temporary morgue was set up in the Horticulture Building at the Ohio State Fairgrounds. Some writers pointed out that exactly a century before a fire had swept through the first Ohio Penitentiary on Scioto Street. And that the doomed west cellblock, added to the original structure in 1875, had been built on ground previously used as a prison cemetery. (CCCJ.)

Fr. Albert O'Brien, the prison's Roman Catholic chaplain, stood on the stairway of cellblocks G and H, giving his "conditional blessing to any soul that might still remain" as the dead and dying were being removed. When he passed away four years later at the age of 45, some 3,500 inmates paid their last respects to the "Hero Priest" as he lay in state inside the prison. (CCCJ.)

Every warden knows (or should know) that to ignore prisoner complaints about the food is to do so at your own peril. However, when your institution is overcrowded and your budget is overextended, the quality of the meals inevitably suffers. This was the situation in "Pentown" (as the inmates had dubbed the prison) on October 31, 1952 at 4:40 p.m., when the so-called "Halloween Riot" erupted. (CCCJ.)

The riot began in the mess hall when inmates began banging on their cups with their spoons. Warden Ralph "Red" Alvis quickly made his way to the scene and addressed the inmates while standing on a table. However, even as he was quelling this disturbance, prisoners in a second mess hall started rioting. Inmates who surrendered or did not participate in the riot are shown being searched. (CCCJ.)

Unable to control the situation, Alvis returned to his office to call the police and Ohio National Guard. In the meantime, some of the prisoners returned to their cells or just sat down in the yard. Others, however, formed gangs to settle the score with other inmates, loot the hospital in search of drugs, or set fire to the buildings (such as this classroom). (CCCJ.)

At 10:00 p.m., a combined force made up of prison staff, the highway patrol, the Columbus Police, and the National Guard stormed the penitentiary, pushing the inmates back into their cellblocks. However, they were unable to secure them in their cells because the inmates had destroyed most of the lock mechanisms and the crash gates in cellblocks G, H, I, and K. (CCCJ.)

On November 3, 1952, with the inmates still in control of their cellblocks, the authorities decided to either "starve or freeze" them out by cutting off all food and heat in the area where 1,600 inmates were housed. A few of them tried to surrender, but the rest began throwing things at the officers, who opened fire. One inmate was killed, four were wounded, and the rest quickly gave up. (CCCJ.)

Following the Halloween riot, the Ohio Highway Patrol was directly involved in the management of the penitentiary for nearly four months. The knowledge it gained about handling such situations—particularly the value of photographs and film, how to deploy troops, knowledge of the institutional layout, experience in handling mobs—was to prove beneficial when faced with a similar riot 16 years later. This was their guardhouse. (CCCJ.)

On June 24, 1968, the population of the Penitentiary was 2,899, or 1,800 fewer than in 1952. Nevertheless Warden E. L. Maxwell was concerned because he had 53 vacant guard positions and morale was low. At about 8:00 a.m., 45 prisoners overran the print shop. Arming themselves with knives, broken bottles, and baseball bats, they took hostages and began setting fire to numerous buildings, causing $1 million in damages. (CCCJ.)

Warden Maxwell was scheduled to retire on July 1 for health reasons. Now, he had a riot on his hands. He called on the Columbus Police, the Ohio Highway Patrol, and the National Guard for assistance, and they quickly responded with rifles, shotguns, sidearms, and fixed bayonets. More than 50 guards and inmates were injured before the situation was brought under control. (CCCJ.)

Following the assassination of Martin Luther King, Jr. on April 4, 1968, rioting had broken out in 110 cities nationwide. Ohio Corrections chief Maury C. Koblentz believed such "outside influences" were instrumental in stirring things up inside the institution. However, Maxwell denied there was any racial unrest within the penitentiary, despite rumors of Black Nationalism and a prison population that was more than half African American. (CCCJ.)

Two days before the riot, an inmate poem was published in the *O.P. News*, reading "Now as I search into tomorrow / War, greed, and sin the world will borrow / As far as I can see; I turn in sorrow." Now, the Treatment Services Building, the auditorium, the print shop, the commissary, the woolen mill, and the cotton mill were smoldering ruins. An inmate is shown climbing out a window. (CCCJ.)

In 1964, funds had been appropriated to build a new prison at Lucasville that would replace the Ohio Penitentiary (as well as a medium security facility at Grafton). However, the death of the landowner delayed construction while his estate was being probated. Furthermore the recent acquisition of the abandoned Federal Reformatory at Chillicothe (former home of Charles Manson) raised doubts about the wisdom of the original plan. (CCCJ.)

On July 5, Marion J. Koloski, the reform-minded warden of the Ohio State Reformatory, was appointed to replace Maxwell, who had been admitted to a hospital with health problems. Nevertheless tensions continued to build throughout July and into August. Finally at 10:15 p.m. on August 20, prisoners seized control of cellblocks C and D at knifepoint, taking nine guards hostage, and then began freeing other prisoners. (CCCJ.)

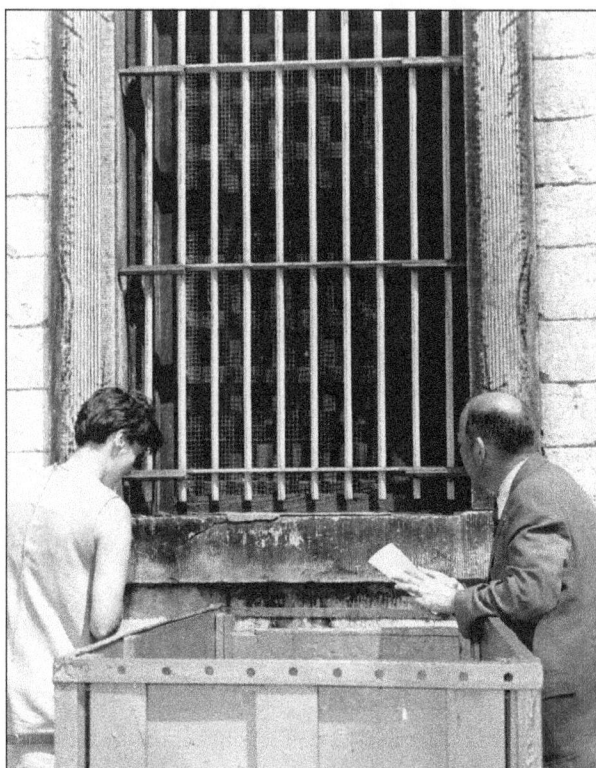

Once again, sporadic fires were set and the mess hall, commissary, and hospital were looted. Warden Marion Koloski received a series of demands calling for several guards to be fired, amnesty for all rioters, increased privileges, and the airing of their grievances to the media. Koloski agreed to all but one of the demands and at 2:00 p.m. allowed the inmates to speak with five members of the media. (CCCJ.)

However, the news conference was stopped after 30 minutes when more violence erupted. It became readily apparent that the riot's leaders had begun fighting among themselves. New demands were issued, along with the threat that they would "burn the hostages to a cinder" and roll a head into the yard if they did not get their way. By that time, some rioters were under the influence of drugs. (CCCJ.)

Five hours into the riot, Gen. Sylvester Del Corso of the National Guard met with Col. Robert Chiaramonte of the highway patrol to devise a rescue plan. As it turned out, Del Corso had dealt with a similar situation in World War II when he recaptured the Manila City Hall from the Japanese. Although Ohio Corrections chief Maury C. Koblentz approved the plan, Koloski still had to give the go-head. (CCCJ.)

Negotiations continued around the clock. But throughout the night, the situation within the prison had steadily deteriorated. Law enforcement officials feared for the safety of the hostages, and with good reason, for at noon on August 21, one inmate stabbed another in clear view of everyone. They could no longer afford to delay the rescue plan. National Guard specialists began to rig the explosive charges. (CCCJ.)

Del Corso's plan involved "shock and speed." Two simultaneous explosions were set off, one on the roof and one on the outside wall of East Hall, momentarily stunning the rioters. Immediately Cpl. V. G. Archer and patrolman S. M. Erter dropped through the hole in the roof to gather up the hostages. At the same time, assault squads entered and secured A-B and C-D blocks and the area between them. (CCCJ.)

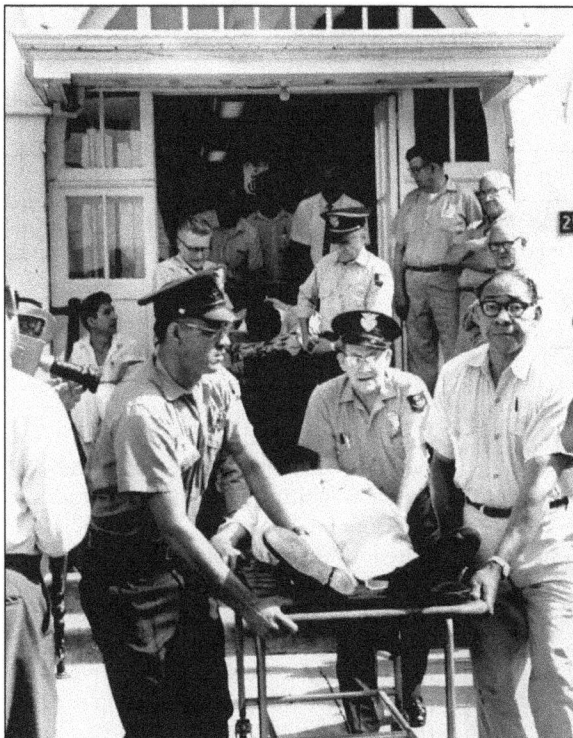

During the riot, three guards, two highway patrol officers, and two Columbus police officers sustained injuries; five inmates had died and nine others were wounded. Apparently in sympathy with the Ohio Penitentiary riot, minor disturbances were also experienced at prisons in London and Lebanon on August 20. These were quickly quashed by the patrol and guard personnel. (CCCJ.)

Three

LITTLE TALES FROM THE BIG HOUSE

The fame or notoriety of a prison derives from a mix of well known "guests" and sensational events. The Ohio Penitentiary had its share of both. For example, there was William Sydney Porter, who wrote under the pen name "O. Henry," and is famous for his "O. Henry endings" or the clever twists in his witty and warm short stories. And there was Chester Himes, a pioneer in the development of African American detective novels with his Harlem-based team of Coffin Ed Johnson and Grave Digger Jones.

While lacking the literary skills of Porter or Himes, Oklahoma train robber Alphonso J. (Al) Jennings wrote several books about his life and was able to parlay his fame as an outlaw into a successful movie career. Another "outlaw" was David Allan Coe, the "Mysterious Rhinestone Cowboy," who served time at the Boys Industrial School, Ohio State Reformatory, and Ohio Penitentiary before making his mark as a songwriter in Nashville.

The "Queen of Ohio," Cassie Chadwick conned banks into loaning her $10 to $20 million by claiming to be Andrew Carnegie's illegitimate daughter. Sentenced to the Ohio Penitentiary on January 1, 1906, Chadwick died there the following year at the age of 50.

On October 12, 1933, henchmen Charles Makley, Harry Pierpont, and Russell Clark entered Lima's Allen County jail and freed John Dillinger after beating Sheriff Jess Sarber to death. Imprisoned in the Ohio Penitentiary, Makley and Pierpont attempted to escape on March 27, 1934, using guns carved out of soapstone. Makley was shot to death, while Pierpont was captured and later executed.

One-time public enemy number six George "Bugs" Moran is best known for having butted heads with Al Capone (and missing the "St. Valentine's Day Massacre"). Following the robbery of a bank messenger in July 1946, which netted $10,000, he was sentenced to the Ohio Penitentiary for 10 years.

And then there was James Brown, the first American "vampire." While working on a whaling ship, Brown, age 25, was accosted by 19-year-old James Foster who called him a racial slur. Brown, the ship's cook, stabbed Foster in the chest and, it is claimed, drank his blood. For his crime, he spent 22 years in the Charleston State Prison, before being transferred to the Ohio Penitentiary on April 14, 1889. Three years later, Brown was removed to a federal insane asylum in Washington, D.C.

GENERAL JOHN H. MORGAN.

In the spring of 1863, Confederate Gen. John Hunt Morgan and a dozen of his officers were sentenced to the Ohio Penitentiary following his abortive raid through southern Ohio. As a prisoner of war, he was not given a number and was treated considerably better than a convicted felon. Meanwhile his troops were incarcerated at nearby Camp Chase Military Prison under much more austere conditions. (RM.)

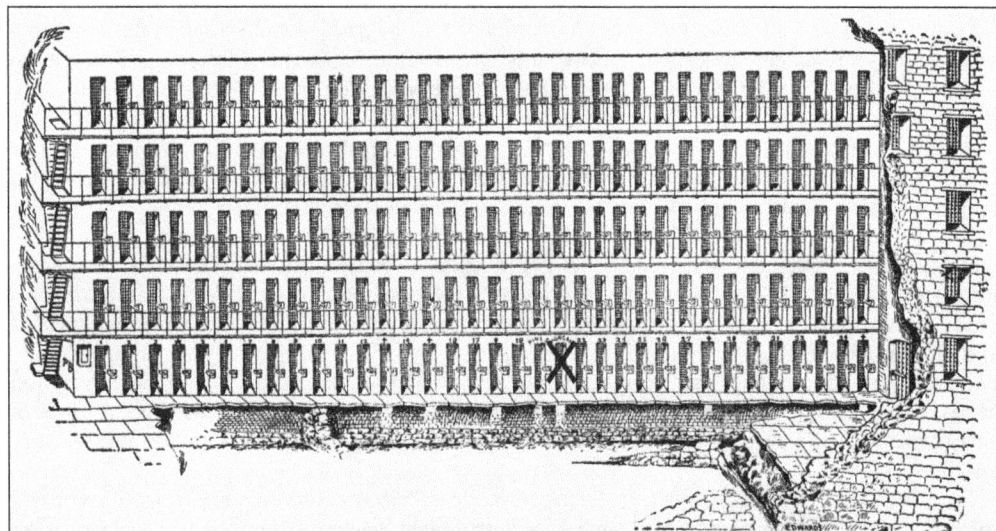

Unwilling to accept his confinement, General Morgan (whose cell is marked with an *x*) and his officers planned to escape by tunneling their way under the cellblock. On the night of November 25, Morgan and his men successfully carried out their plan, although there is reason to believe they were assisted by so-called "copperhead" sympathizers to the southern cause on the prison staff. (Authors' collection.)

Up until new cells were installed in 1909, cell 21 in the old East Hall was a popular feature of any Ohio Penitentiary tour. Although it was purchased by Kentucky businessman John A. Kelley for shipment to the John Hunt Morgan Memorial in Lexington, there is no record of it ever arriving, according to David Roth, publisher of Columbus-based *Blue & Gray* magazine. (CML.)

In *The Life Story of Sarah M. Victor*, Sarah Victor (shown in her cell) relates how she was falsely convicted of poisoning her brother for his life insurance and subsequently spent 19 years at the Ohio Penitentiary until she was pardoned on Christmas Day, 1886. Her misfortune, however, allowed her to produce a good description of life in the "Female Department" of the penitentiary during the administration of several early wardens. (Authors' collection.)

The "girls" (as the female prisoners were generally called) are shown in the dining room of the annex where they were supervised by the principal matron. On the right side are four cells. According to Sarah Victor, the position of matron was "a hard one to hold long creditably, for when once a matron is overpowered by a prisoner or censured by the warden," her usefulness is over. (Authors' collection.)

A building for female prisoners had been built in 1837, just east of the main building. It contained 11 cells and various workrooms for the women to ply their trades. Typical work assignments included the laundry, sewing room, and dining room, but, as this illustration of chair-making shows, they also undertook other tasks when there was sufficient workspace and the necessary resources. (Authors' collection.)

Warden Elijah G. Coffin wrote to Victor following her release, saying "You speak of my kindness to you during the time you was under my charge, with appreciation. I presume I was no more kind than former wardens, and I presume, also, that at no time was you more kindly treated than your conduct merited, for your own sake and for the good influence you had over the inmates." (Authors' collection.)

On April 25, 1898, William Sidney Porter arrived at the Ohio Penitentiary. A federal judge in Texas sentenced the 33-year-old alcoholic bookkeeper to five years for embezzlement. Released three years, two months, and 27 days later, inmate number 30664 was soon to become one of the most famous short story writers of all times, O. Henry. Some of his characters were based on people he met in prison. (CCCJ.)

While confined at the prison, William Sidney Porter worked in the hospital and began writing short stories. Some of these he managed to smuggle out of the institution where they were forwarded to a publisher. Despite his success, he died an alcoholic in New York a dozen years later. In 1907, he drew this ironic sketch of his friend, Al Jennings (who believed he never overcame his prison experiences). (Authors' collection.)

In *Through The Shadows With O. Henry*, Al Jennings wrote of his friendship with the world-famous writer, both in and out of prison. He had been a prosecuting attorney in Oklahoma before he turned to crime as the leader of a band of fumbling desperados called the "Jennings Gang." As it turned out, Jennings was much more successful as a movie cowboy and technical advisor on Hollywood westerns. (Authors' collection.)

42

John Henry Sloan was known as the "O.P. Freak" because he walked on "all fours like an animal." Convicted of counterfeiting in South Carolina, he was sentenced to the penitentiary for three and a half years. Sloan is quoted as having said, "I have been terribly crooked in my life, I will say that, and I will say further that I haven't done a straight act in twenty years." (Authors' collection.)

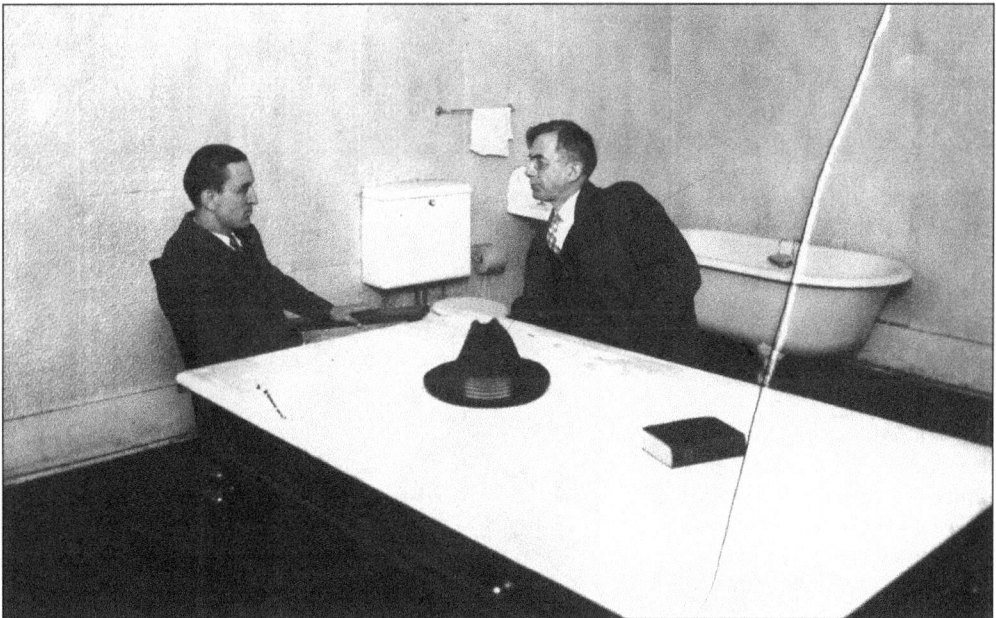

In 1926, Jacob Nesbitt (on left) of Troy bludgeoned and strangled his wife, Frances, to death because she "nagged" him and was convicted of second-degree murder. Upon arriving at the penitentiary, Nesbitt purportedly became warden Preston Thomas's "pet" because he and the warden's son were fraternity brothers. As a result, Nesbitt was free to roam the city, spending time at Ohio State University, and eating in local restaurants. (CCCJ.)

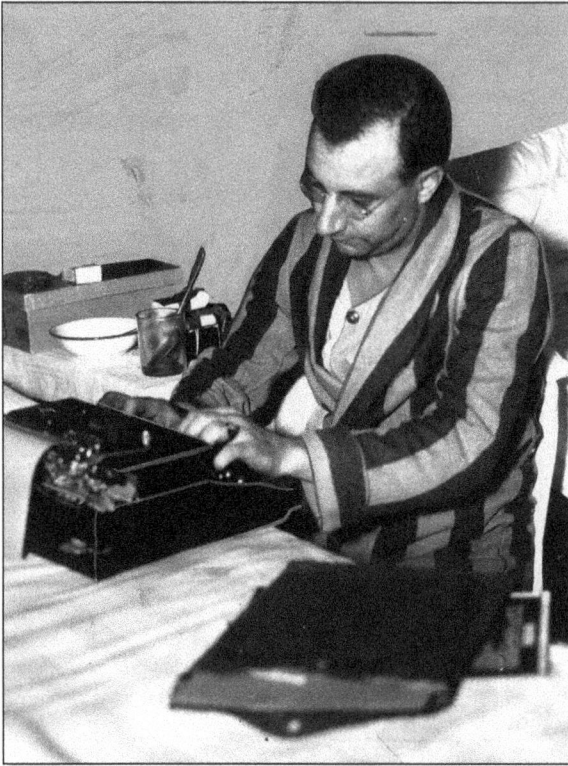

Although his parents had hoped he would become a priest, Thomas "Yonnie" Licavoli garnered his first arrest at age 12. More would follow. While AWOL from the U.S. Navy, Licavoli settled in Detroit where he was befriended by mob boss "Singing Sam" Cantalonotte, joined the notorious Purple Gang, and steadily built up his criminal organization through judiciously applied brutality. He then set his sights on Ohio. (CCCJ.)

Even by Detroit's standards, Licavoli's tactics were exceptionally vicious. When Toledo bootlegger John Kennedy refused to knuckle under, Licavoli ordered a hit on the troublesome Irishman. On July 7, 1933, Kennedy was gunned down while walking on the beach with his girlfriend. Licavoli was sentenced to life in prison for the murder of Kennedy and three other rivals, although some maintain he was framed. (CCCJ.)

Licavoli served 37 years in the Ohio Penitentiary before he was paroled in 1971. In a controversial move, Gov. James A. Rhodes had reduced his charge to second-degree murder. While in prison, Licavoli was suspected of corrupting more than one warden, receiving special privileges. Following his release, he ran a stamp-collecting store, started, some inmates claimed, with stamps removed from century-old prison files. (CCCJ.)

In 1899, John B. C. Eckstrom was hired away from Kenyon College to coach football at Ohio State University and in his first season the team went undefeated. However, two years later he resigned to take the coaching job at Ohio Medical College, having compiled a record of 23 wins, 4 losses, and 3 ties. By 1940, Dr. Eckstrom was working as the physician at the Ohio Penitentiary. (CCCJ.)

Inmate Clarence Doss stands before his portrait of Mrs. John Eckstrom, wife of the prison physician, completed in 1940. During his years of confinement, Doss taught himself how to paint from studying books he bought with his meager earnings in his prison job. He became quite adept at working from photographs, and his fame spread beyond the prison walls. He first garnered attention for his 1931 painting of Jesus. (CCCJ.)

As an expatriate in Paris, Chester Himes achieved the literary acclaim that had eluded him back home. Expelled from Ohio State University because of a "prank," Himes turned to crime and at 19 was sentenced to the Ohio Penitentiary for armed robbery. After the 1930 fire, he began writing stories modeled on the pulp fiction of Dashiell Hammett. His best-known novel is *Cotton Comes To Harlem*. (LOC.)

Early on the morning of July 4, 1954, Marilyn Sheppard of Bay Village, Ohio, was savagely beaten to death. Her husband, Dr. Samuel Sheppard, was convicted of second-degree murder and sentenced to life in prison. His motive was thought to be a three-year affair with a nurse. However, Dr. Sheppard insisted he had struggled with a bushy-haired man who entered their home and knocked him unconscious. (CCCJ.)

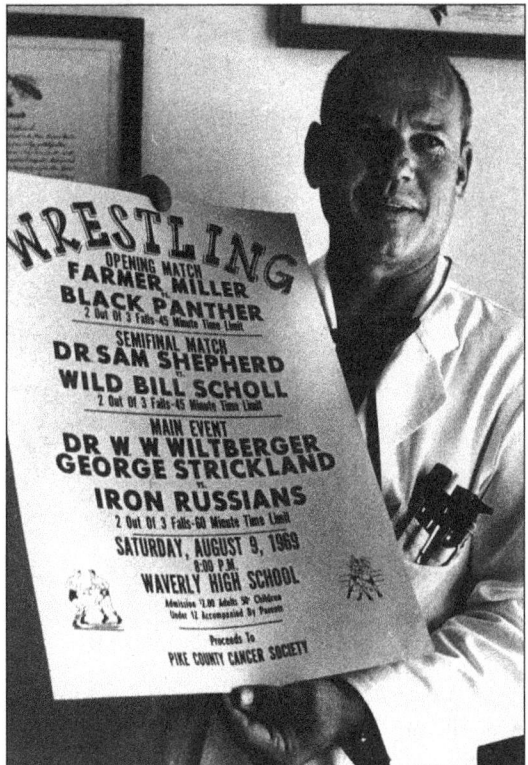

Sheppard was the poster child for media bias. A newspaper headline famously asked, "Why Isn't Sam Sheppard In Jail?" After he served almost a decade in prison, a U.S. district overturned his conviction, and the U.S. Supreme Court ruled that due to the "carnival atmosphere," he had been denied a fair trial. *The Fugitive*, a popular 1963–1967 television series (and 1993 movie), was inspired by the Sheppard case. (CCCJ.)

In 1966, Dr. Samuel Sheppard was acquitted in a new trial. During his imprisonment, both his mother and a brother committed suicide and his father died of cancer. He was briefly married to Ariane Tebbenjohanns (shown), a German divorcee, who had taken up his cause while he was in prison, and then married the 20-year-old daughter of George Strickland, his wrestling mentor. He died of liver failure in 1970. (CCCJ.)

Pictured is the inmate coaching staff of the Ohio Penitentiary Hurricanes. They are, from left to right, Charlie Starling (backfield), Sam Sheppard (trainer), Fred Grambo (trainer), George Goring (line), Ted Kramer (backfield), and Walter Swyers (head). A feared opponent in both football and softball, the Hurricanes had a reputation for playing "clean and hard, real hard" (according to Maj. Grover Powell). When at home, they played on O. Henry Field. (CCCJ.)

Experience: What you get when you're expecting something else.	**Ohio Penitentiary News** *64th Year of Publication*	Diplomacy: The art of letting someone have your way.

Volume 64   Columbus 15, Ohio, Saturday, May 19, 1956   Number 5

CANCER RESEARCH
VOLUNTEERS NEEDED

For many years there has existed, one of many puzzling phenomena in the growth of cancer cells that still needs an answer; is still unsolved. Live cancer cells can be transferred from one individual to another. In the person who has cancer, the cancer cells will live and grow. In the person who has no cancer in his body, all of the transferred cells will die, eventually, after a short period of growth. It is this part of the problem that requires some further observation and study. Just how the normal individual who does not have cancer, can kill off the transplanted "Foreign" cancer cells, is the present important problem. So far, in past experiments, all attempts at growing one person's cancer cells in another individual, who does not have cancer, have ultimately failed. This is so, definitely, as far as we know now, that if transplanted cells do not grow, when injected into another person, it follows, that the injected person does not have cancer. If the cells do grow,

skin. At the end of a two week period, one of the injection sites would be entirely removed by a surgical excision, of the injected area. The injection site in the other forearm, would be observed for an—as yet—undetermined, period of time, and then later be surgically removed. The study of these skin biopsies—it is hoped—would bring forth some information on how the normal or non-cancerous individual's body-reaction goes about it's normal process of "killing-off" these foreign cancer cells that have been transplanted into it.

The only hospitalization required would be for the overnight stays, following the biopsies (surgical excision of the injected areas).

Inmates with any type of known illness (diabetes, quiescent Tb, syphillis, osteomyelitis, peptic ulcer, heart trouble, high-blood-pressure, etc.,) would be accept-able as volunteers for cancer research.

In 1956, the Sloan Kettering Institute and the Ohio State University College of Medicine collaborated on a study in which they injected live cancer cells just under the skin on the arms of inmate volunteers to see whether they could develop an immunity. They only asked for 25, but 120 inmates stepped forward, hoping to be able to do something good for society. (CCCJ.)

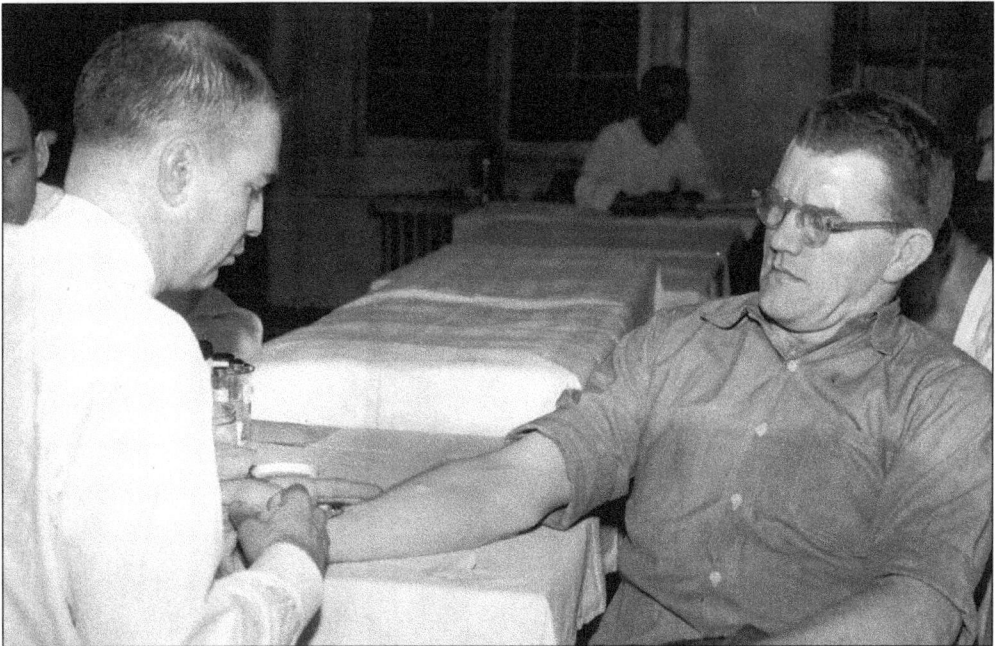

Dr. Chester M. Southam, the lead researcher, later was accused of violating medical ethics when he failed to obtain informed consent from some elderly and senile patients at the Jewish Chronic Disease Hospital in a similar study. Unfortunately he also failed to do any real follow up with the Ohio Penitentiary subjects so the value of his research (and the inmates' sacrifice) is questionable. (CCCJ.)

49

John Weber died at the Ohio Penitentiary in early 1976, after spending 50 years behind bars. At the time of his death, he was the oldest inmate in the world at almost 100. Nearly blind, he was often shown celebrating his September 24 birthday behind bars. Convicted of second-degree murder, this immigrant from Austro-Hungary repeatedly turned down parole because he would have been deported. (CCCJ.)

In 1971, alto sax player Logan Rollins was looking for a way to make doing hard time a little easier. So he put together the Ohio Penitentiary 511 Jazz Ensemble to play to their captive audience (with guest vocalist Robert "Singin' Sam" Taylor). The following year, the group recorded an album, *Hard Luck Soul*, which was sold in the prison gift shop and became something of a collector's item. (Authors' collection.)

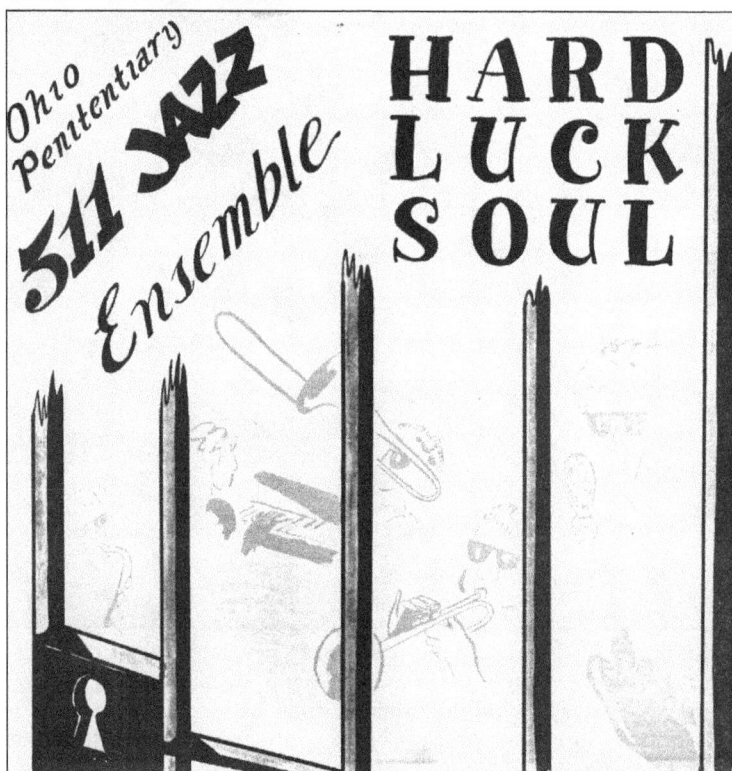

Four

THE PALACE OF DEATH

In 1885, the state legislature passed a bill authorizing all court-ordered executions to take place at the Ohio Penitentiary. Previously anyone sentenced to death was publicly hanged in the county where the crime occurred. Valentine Wagner holds the dubious honor of being the first man to die on the gallows at the penitentiary when he was hanged on July 31, 1885, for the murder of his brother-in-law Daniel Shehan in Morrow County.

Over the next decade, 27 more men were hanged at the Ohio Penitentiary before the electric chair was introduced in 1897 as a more humane form of execution. At 17 years old, William Haas of Hamilton County, who had raped and murdered Mrs. William Brady, was the first to die in this manner.

During the period 1897 to 1963, 314 more passed through the "Goodbye Door" (as the door to the Death House was called), including three women. The first was serial killer Anna Marie Hahn of Cincinnati who was put to death on December 7, 1938, for poisoning at least four men. The last was Betty Evelyn Butler, also of Cincinnati, who had strangled and drowned a woman who had befriended her. She died on June 11, 1954. The last man executed at the penitentiary was Donald Reinbolt, on March 15, 1963, for the murder of Edgar L. Weaver, a Columbus grocer.

When the U.S. Supreme Court declared the death penalty unconstitutional in 1972, the 65 inmates then occupying death row had their sentences commuted to life in prison. Convicted murderers who had every reason to believe they were going to be put to death suddenly had hopes of eventually being paroled. Meanwhile death row was officially relocated to the newly opened Southern Ohio Correctional Facility at Lucasville.

In August 1984, following an eight-month reprieve, the Ohio Penitentiary was finally closed by order of U.S. District Court Judge Robert Duncan, having received its own "death sentence" on December 31, 1983.

After the 1968 riot, Gov. James A. Rhodes had started the ball rolling with the construction of a replacement facility in Lucasville. When it was completed in 1972, most of the inmates were transferred there, but the Ohio Penitentiary continued to operate as a medical facility, housing "the sick and infirm, the psychotic and the troublemakers." Despite the fact that the buildings were literally falling apart, the facility continued to be used for a dozen more years.

As far as anyone knows, Esther Foster was the first woman hanged in Ohio. While at the penitentiary, she was convicted of beating another prisoner to death with a shovel. Foster was executed in Columbus on February 9, 1844, after donating her body to a surgeon for all the candy she could eat. Sharing the gallows was inmate William Graham, who had killed a prison guard with an axe. (Authors' collection.)

In *The Palace of Death or The Ohio Penitentiary Annex*, author H. M. Fogle provided short biographies of everyone who was executed in the prison through 1907. This photograph of the "Death Chamber" shows the location of the trapdoor of the gallows directly above the electric chair. On the other side of the brick wall was the "Death Cage" where the condemned man was confined prior to his execution. (Authors' collection.)

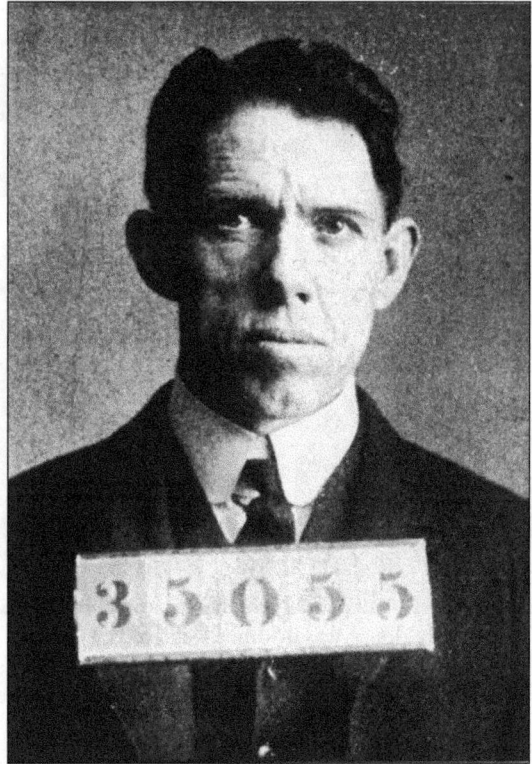

Shortly after midnight on November 25, 1904, Otis E. Loveland was strapped into the electric chair and 1,750 volts of electricity coursed through his body, but he did not die. The charge was administered a second time, and still his heart continued to beat. It was not until the third application that Loveland finally expired, put to death for the murder of George Geyer, an elderly farmer. (Authors' collection.)

Death Chamber, Ohio Penitentiary, Columbus, Ohio.

Inmate carpenter Harry Glick is credited with making the original electric chair in 1897. Contrary to legend, however, he did not die in it. Rather Charles Justice, also known as Jackson, who improved the restraint system by replacing leather straps with metal clamps, did. A decade following his release from the penitentiary, Justice was convicted of a robbery and murder and was put to death in the chair on November 27, 1911. (WF.)

53

The Death House was originally called the "Annex" and was housed at the far end of "Old Hall" (or East Hall), which were the first cellblocks constructed (A, B, C, and D). These cells were narrower and very poorly ventilated. Eventually they were all replaced (including Gen. John H. Morgan's cell). In 1913, a separate Death House was constructed. This is Death Row as it appeared in 1952. (CCCJ.)

William Haas, the "Boy Murderer," was the first person electrocuted in Ohio when he was executed on April 21, 1897, at the age of 17. Orphaned, friendless, and illiterate, he was hired by William Brady of Cincinnati to help him with the chores around his suburban home. One morning without warning, Haas forced himself upon Mrs. Brady and then nearly severed her head with a razor when she threatened to tell her husband. (Authors' collection.)

Five minutes after Haas was executed, William Wiley, also of Cincinnati, was strapped into the same chair and 1,750 volts of electricity coursed through his body. A bad tempered man, Wiley had shot his wife to death during a drinking spree. He and Haas, whom he did not like, were made to flip a coin to see who would die first. Wiley "won," gaining a five-minute reprieve. (Authors' collection.)

Columbus's bid for "Crime of the Century" occurred on June 14, 1929, when two teenage boys found the body of 29-year-old Theora Hix at a rifle range on Fisher Road near McKinley Avenue. She had been beaten and stabbed. Initially Marion Meyers, an ex-boyfriend, was suspected, but when his alibi checked out suspicion fell on Dr. James Howard Snook, former head of the Ohio State University Department of Veterinary Medicine. (CCCJ.)

Married with a wife and young daughter, Dr. James Howard Snook was connected to Theora Hix by the manager of a Hubbard Avenue "love nest" where the two had been having an affair for three years. They first met when she was a student and Snook was a distinguished, if rather unassuming, member of the faculty who had won a gold medal in pistol shooting at the 1920 Olympics. (CCCJ.)

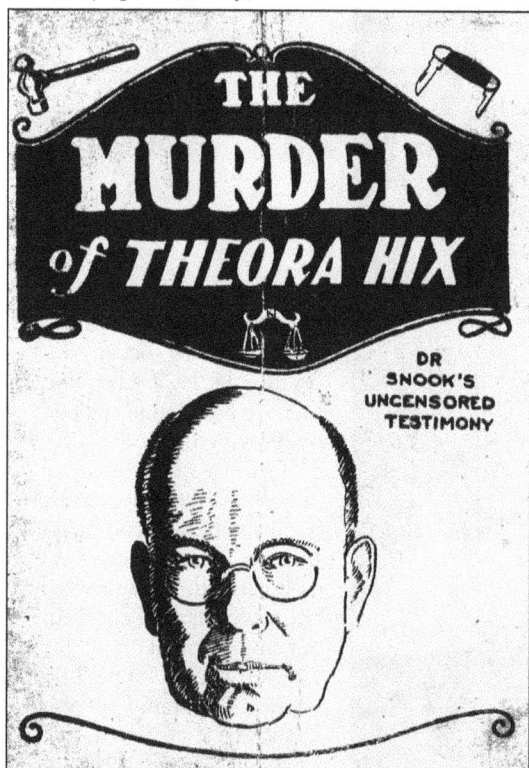

The trial attracted nationwide attention with top writers from around the country assigned to report the salacious details—at least as many of them as the newspapers at the time could print. This booklet of court testimony was quickly published to satisfy the demand for information on how the jazz age "wild girl" Hix had seduced and corrupted the respected professor with a mix of sex and drugs. (Authors' collection.)

All that is known for certain is that the whole matter came to a climax when Dr. Snook killed Hix in his car with a ball peen hammer and a pocket knife, purportedly because she was jealous of his time away from her. The trial lasted 30 days, but the jury took just 28 minutes to find him guilty. He was remanded to the Ohio Penitentiary and put to death in the electric chair on February 28, 1930. (CCCJ.)

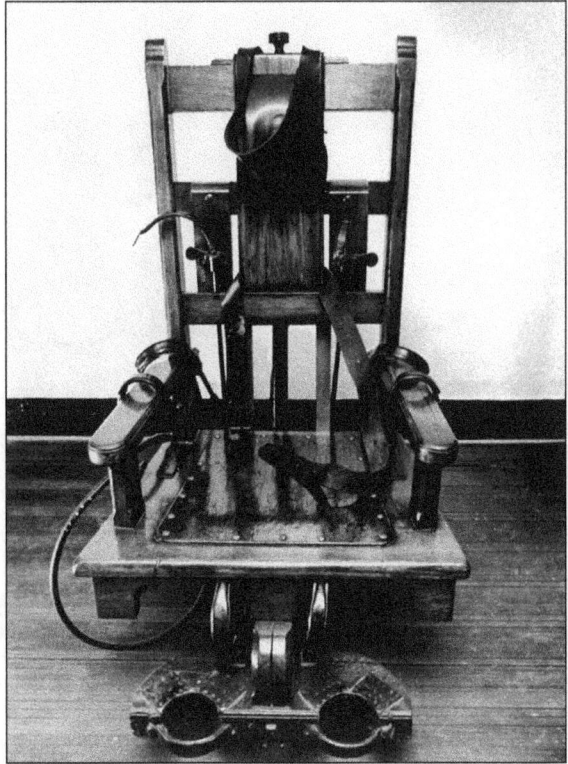

When Blanche "Dovie" Dean's 68-year-old husband of five months, Hawkins, died from ingesting rat poison, the 55-year-old grandmother and widow first tried to blame her stepson, before accusing her own son from an earlier marriage. She finally admitted after failing a lie detector test that she had done it herself, but only because she feared for her own life. Blanche claimed that life with her new husband had been unbearable. (CCCJ.)

57

The day before their wedding, Hawkins Dean had made Dovie the sole beneficiary of his $27,000 estate, including his 115-acre farm in Batavia, Ohio. The police suspected that this may have been the only motive Dovie needed, although she told Clermont County sheriff Clyde B. Dericks, "I got him before he got me." She put arsenic in his milk on four separate occasions. (CCCJ.)

Married three times before, Dovie testified that Hawkins could not adequately perform his "husbandly duties," and that this had led to several, increasingly violent arguments in which, finally, he threatened to kill her. Clearly they had different expectations from the marriage; she wanted a home, and he wanted a housekeeper. Judged to be sane, she was found guilty with no recommendation of mercy after only 40 minutes. (CCCJ.)

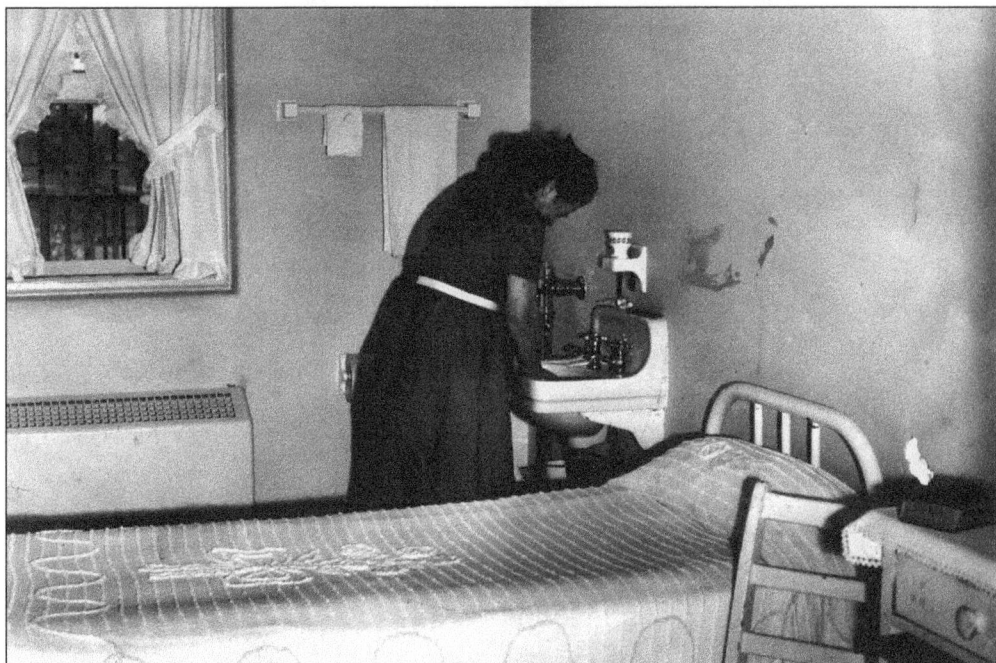

While confined at the Ohio Reformatory for Women in Marysville, Dovie Dean kept a parakeet named Charlie. She was then moved to the Ohio Penitentiary where, on January 15, 1954, an extremely calm Dovie became the second women to die in the electric chair. Anna Marie Hahn, the Cincinnati poisoner, had been the first. The day before Dovie's execution, she had her hair done. (CCCJ.)

The "Death House" was a modest, one-story brick building with two doors and one small window in front and two small, mesh-covered windows on the side. It housed "Old Sparky," inmates' nickname for the electric chair, and a "Rogues' Gallery," a collection of portraits of executed criminals. It was built in two weeks in 1927 specifically to house the electric chair, replacing another one, which dated back to 1913. (CCCJ.)

In 1913, John Atkinson, a Cuyahoga county prisoner, conducted a scientific experiment of sorts in the "Death Chamber" by raising canaries and teaching them to sing using a phonograph. Similarly in 1968, inmate-turned-novelist Robert McKay, while serving as the custodian of the electric chair in the Death House, used the space to breed red factor canaries. His semi-autobiographical novel, *Canary Red*, was published the same year. (CCCJ.)

Although he allowed six executions to proceed while he was governor, Michael V. Disalle was an opponent of the death penalty and co-founded the National Committee to Abolish Federal Death Penalty after failing to win a second term. His 1965 book, *The Power of Life and Death*, discusses his personal struggles over whether to commute a death sentence. He believed it was mostly exacted on the poor. (CCCJ.)

In 1971, Phil Donahue originated a weeklong broadcast of his syndicated television show live from the Ohio Penitentiary. The fifth episode took place in the Death House and included interviews with two inmates who had been sentenced to death. Here Donahue is seen contemplating "Old Thunderbolt," another nickname for the chair. Donahue has argued that the media has a right to broadcast all executions. (CCCJ.)

On August 27, 1957, Paul Coblentz, a 25-year-old Amish farmer in Mount Hope, was robbed of $9 by two men, Eugene Peters and Michael Doumoulin, who picked his home at random. When they started to assault his wife, Dora (who was protecting their 17-month-old child), Paul tried to summon help and was gunned down by Peters as he ran out the door. This was the murder site. (CCCJ.)

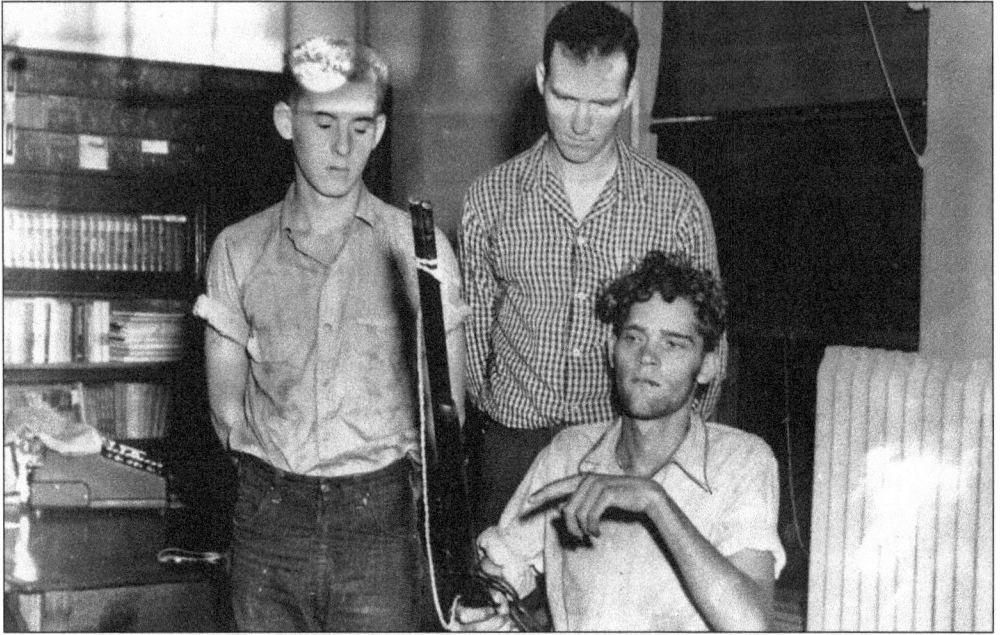

Eugene Peters and Michael Doumoulin fled the scene in a stolen truck, later switching to a stolen car. Arriving in Illinois, they broke a pane out of the window of a hunting cabin and climbed some boards to hide inside. However, they were located by a country constable and tried to shoot their way out with a hunting rifle before surrendering to police. Here they are with the murder weapon. (CCCJ.)

Peters was found guilty of the murder of Paul Coblentz and was sentenced to die in the electric chair. However, the Amish community deluged the governor's office with letters asking for clemency. None of them, including Moses Coblentz, Paul's father, wanted Peters executed in their name. They even viewed his parents as fellow victims. Just seven hours before the scheduled execution, the governor commuted the condemned man's sentence. (CCCJ.)

During the ensuing trial in Holmes County, journalists profiled a culture that, until then, few people in the country knew about. They were particularly intrigued that the Amish expressed no hatred of the two men and had no desire to seek vengeance against them. Although Moses felt grief over his son's death, he went to visit Peters in jail and told him, "I hope God can forgive you." (CCCJ.)

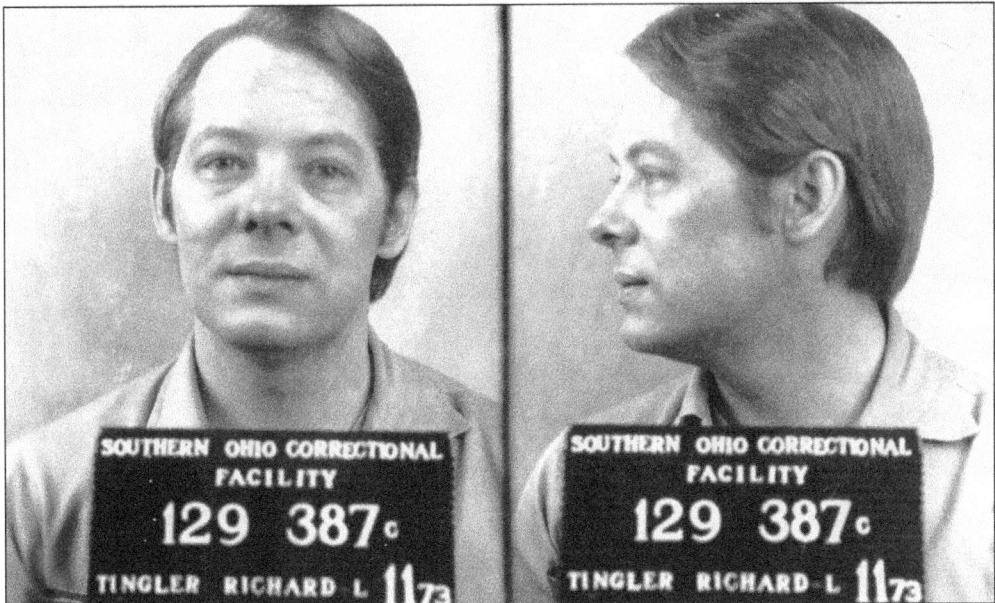

Lest anyone forget why prisons exist, there is always Richard Lee Tingler Jr. Between September 1968 and April 1969, Tingler viciously murdered six people in the course of committing two robberies in Cleveland and Columbus, earning him a spot on the FBI's 10 Most Wanted list. Arrested in Oklahoma, Tingler was sentenced to death (commuted to life when the U.S. Supreme Court overturned the death penalty). (CCCJ.)

Jurors for the Richard Lee Tingler Jr. trial are seen visiting the murder scene. After beating her co-workers to death, Tingler tried to strangle Phyllis Crow with a coat hanger. That was on October 20, 1968. Unable to return to work due to her injuries, Crow lived in fear for the next 26 years. It was not until Tingler died of cancer on March 18, 1995, that her nightmare was finally over. (CCCJ.)

On June 16, 1985, Columbus rock and roll "oldies" band Phil Dirt and the Dozers rented the unoccupied Ohio Penitentiary for a "Jailhouse Rock" concert. Some 5,000 people crowded into the old prison to see the band and tour the grounds. The Dozers subsequently released a live recording of the concert. For the Ohio Penitentiary, it was truly "the last dance." It was demolished in March 1997. (Authors' collection.)

Five

FROM REFUGE TO
REFORM SCHOOL

The Ohio Reform School (or Farm) was established by an act of the Ohio General Assembly on April 16, 1857, with Charles Reemelin of Cincinnati, John A. Foot of Cleveland, and James D. Ladd of Steubenville named its first commissioners. Hovever, a bill introduced by James Monroe of Oberlin to appropriate $1,000 to defray the cost of sending the commissioners to evaluate the other institutions was defeated.

Although many had a hand in creating the Ohio Reform Farm, Reemelin provided "the beautiful plan." A German by birth, he came to America as a youth and soon acquired fame and fortune in his adoptive country. More than anyone else, he was determined that the Ohio Reform Farm would not be just another prison.

Up until then, the State of Ohio locked up male juvenile offenders with adult criminals in the Ohio Penitentiary. After visiting many of the existing institutions for youth in the United States, Reemelin travelled to England, France, and Germany at his own expense to inspect their facilities.

Inspired by France's Colonie de Mettray, Reemelin returned to Ohio determined to model the Ohio Reform Farm on the "family" or "cottage" system. The decision was made to establish the institution on 1,210 acres approximately six miles south of Lancaster in the rolling hills of Fairfield County.

Reemelin opened the Ohio Reform Farm in 1858 with 12 boys from the Cincinnati House of Refuge. The Ohio General Assembly had specified that up to 40 boys drawn from the House of Refuge, the Ohio Penitentiary, and the county jails of the state should constitute the first family.

George E. Howe became acting commissioner of the school following Reemelin's departure and remained as superintendent for 19 years. He was responsible for providing the facility with direction and consistency, ensuring that it did not stray for the course that had been set by his predecessor. He also was an outspoken evangelist of "the Family System" on a national level, helping to establish similar institutions around the country.

It was frequently noted that "The Ohio reform [farm] showed the value of a permanent board of managers, having been under the direction of the same board from the start. No removal from office had ever been made, and no changes except by resignation." Consequently, by 1901, 28 states had established similar facilities.

Opened on October 7, 1850, the Cincinnati House of Refuge was a four-story stone building surrounded by a high wall. Boys and girl from ages 6 to 19 could be committed to it by their parents, guardians, the masters to whom they had been apprenticed, or the court system. The most common offenses were vagrancy, petty larceny, incorrigibility, and running away. By 1915, the facility had closed. (Authors' collection.)

Col. John C. Hite succeeded George E. Howe as superintendent of the institution in 1878, when the latter took charge of the State Reform School of Connecticut in Meriden. Hite, from Lancaster, had been a farmer, teacher, bookseller, and county auditor before being appointed superintendent. He was addressed by the boys as "Brother," which was the term of respect used for all officers of the institution. (Authors' collection.)

Ohio Reform Farm commissioner B. W. Chidlaw's attitude was typical of the era (1871): "We are fully persuaded . . . that the human heart is sinful and prone to evil; and this we find true of the inmates of the Ohio reform farm school. Their wills are stubborn; their passions ungoverned; their appetites depraved; their understanding darkened; their heads, hearts and hands alienated from God and his law." (Authors' collection.)

Henry Howe, father of Ohio history, visited the Boys' Industrial School, as it was later called, and noted, "From 1858 to 1885, a period of twenty-seven years, out of 4,530 boys who have been here there have been but twenty-three deaths, four of these by accident." He concluded it must be one of the healthiest spots on earth. This print was made from a photograph taken by Howe. (Authors' collection.)

1. MAIN BUILDING.
2. FAMILY BUILDINGS.
3. WOOD HOUSE.
4. SHOPS.

OHIO REFORM SCH

5. BAKE HOUSE.
6. LOCK UP.
7. WASH ROOM.

This rare print shows the Ohio Reform Farm in 1870. Starting clockwise at left are two cottages with a washhouse between them, then the wood house, followed by the workshops. Next is the main building in the middle. Behind it to the left is the bake house and to the right is a lock-up. All of the remaining buildings on the right side are cottages. In 1885, the "Chamber of Reflection" (lock-up) was abandoned, but the "rod" was used for punishment whenever necessary. Col. John C. Hite felt that physical isolation and security wards were of no value and that corporal punishment only had a temporary impact. So under his system, he gave each boy the same number of demerits to work off when he arrived, regardless of his offense. The Disciplinary Unit was responsible for planting thousands of trees. (BIS/FSB.)

From left to right are the feed mill, dairy barn, and Scioto and Pattison Cottages. Henry Howe wrote that the success of the Ohio Reform Farm brought in "a better class of farmers" while "pushing out the rude population yet dwelling in cabins, and called by the boys 'hillikens.' The 'hillikens' are the police of the institution, and ever ready to 'nab' a runaway for the standing reward of $5." (BIS/FSB.)

The "Dinky," a small train, shuttled passengers back and forth from Lancaster to the Boys' Industrial School (BIS) eight times a day (nine on Sundays). The tracks were laid by work crews from the institution, who also built the BIS Road that winds its way to town through the hilly countryside. The railroad ended at the institutional power plant, which supplied steam heat and direct current to the institution. (BIS/FSB.)

The cottages, as the family buildings or residences were called, originally bore the names of Ohio waterways: Muskingum, Ohio, Hocking, Scioto, Cuyahoga, Huron, Maumee, Miami, and Erie. The family of boys living in each building was referred to by the name of the cottage, such as the Maumee family, Hocking family, and so on. Later cottages were named for Ohio governors or other political figures. In 1877, there was discussion regarding the separation of the older and younger boys. The newly constructed Ohio Cottage, with a designed capacity of 100, was intended to be the start of a new institution for younger boys. This concept was later developed through the establishment of the Ohio Youth Commission in 1963. One such institution was the Herbert F. Christian Youth Camp, named after a war hero and Congressional Medal of Honor recipient from Byesville, Ohio, who had spent time at the Boys' Industrial School as a youth. (BIS/FSB.)

Until 1956, the cottages were segregated by race. For example, Harris and Pattison were at one time restricted to African American youth. By the 1970s, however, the boys were being classified by Interpersonal Maturity Level ("I-Level") for treatment purposes, but the results were often the same as one cottage might consist of (African American) youth from the inner city and another (white) youth from rural areas. (BIS/FSB.)

The conservatory, or greenhouse (shown in 1908), was famous for its plants, including what was once the only banana tree in Ohio. The Ridgeview Garden Club held an annual plant sale that attracted buyers from all over the region. Plants cultivated at the Boys' Industrial School were routinely used to decorate the governor's mansion in Columbus both inside and out. (BIS/FSB.)

Jennings Hall (or the armory) was named for Malcolm Jennings, a trustee of the Boys' Industrial School. The first floor was used for drill practice, the second floor had a basketball court with a balcony, and the basement contained the first indoor swimming pool in the state. Many popular entertainers such as the Ink Spots performed there. Built in 1896, this photograph is from 1908. (BIS/FSB.)

Located between Hocking and Lagonda Cottages, the Protestant Chapel, built in 1896, was also used as a movie theater every Sunday. It was open to anyone in the community and people would come from miles around. The stained glass window was removed and shipped to Columbus when the chapel was razed. Recently it was discovered that the window had been installed in a room of the governor's mansion. (BIS/FSB.)

From left to right are Nash, Harmon A and B, Erie (Huron), and Maumee Cottages, and the Central or North School. Cottage officers, teachers, instructors, and others who had boys under their supervision were allowed to place a boy "on line" for minor misconduct. The boy had to stand upright and apart from whatever activity he might have been involved in, although no strained positions were permitted. (BIS/FSB.)

A brick horse barn was built by the boys in 1891 to replace one that had burned down two years earlier with the loss of 12 horses. The sewage filter beds were so bad at this time that the area below the barn was known as "Bean Soup Hollow," and there was a typhoid fever epidemic in 1897. The barn stood empty for many years. (CCCJ.)

74

Formerly the administration building and home of the superintendent, this magnificent structure (shown in 1922) was converted into Dixon Honor Dorm. Beds were set-up in the hallways on the second floor, a dozen or so in each wing. The boys who were studying to be barbers lived here and enjoyed other privileges as well. The center of the mansion (which still survives) is surmounted by a stain glass dome. (CCCJ.)

Originally each cottage had its own schoolroom. But over time, it became necessary to construct an actual school building. The Main School (shown in 1922) was also known as the North School and functioned much as a junior high. Later East School, catering to the younger boys, and Reemelin High School were added. Considerable effort was invested in providing the youth with a good education. (BIS/FSB.)

Named after a Springfield creek (which also lent its name to a British automobile manufactured by Wilbur Gunn), Lagonda Cottage is shown as it looked in 1922 when it was 23 years old. This cottage was where the institution's musicians were housed. In fact, musical symbols were part of the architectural decoration of the building. In 1929, Lagonda Cottage was used as a hospital ward during the influenza epidemic. (CCCJ.)

In this 1939 photograph, the large building in the foreground is Bushnell Cottage. Immediately behind it to the left is the hospital. In 1904, the institution was allocated $15,000 for a hospital. However, there had been a "hospital" (or "pest house") of some sort since at least 1889. During the 1918 influenza epidemic, 16 women from the Ohio Reformatory for Women were sent here as nurses. (BIS/FSB.)

The first floor of this building housed the storeroom, and on the second floor was the tailor shop. Outside the storeroom was a scale for weighing trucks to ensure the institution received full measure for its purchases. However, the scale was also used to weigh teams of boys to make sure they were of equal weight for the annual tug-of-war. The building was located next to the barber shop. (BIS/FSB.)

Bushnell Cottage (shown in 1946) was named after Asa Smith Bushnell of Springfield, who succeeded William McKinley as governor, serving two terms. The cottage was built in 1897 while Bushnell was still in office, probably to curry political favor. The design was copied for an institution in Kentucky. In typical government fashion, a $60,000 roof was installed on the cottage a mere two years before it was torn down. (CCCJ.)

In his 1950 expose, *Our Rejected Children*, Albert Deutsch labeled the Boys' Industrial School a "Big Institutional Slum." He noted that it had the largest population of the 90-odd training schools for child offenders nationwide. As a result, chronic overcrowding undermined even the best-intentioned treatment efforts. More than 40 percent of the youth did not receive schooling and only 10–15 percent attended classes daily. The state legislature had failed to appropriate the necessary funds to correct the problems everyone knew existed. As early as 1866, eight years after it first opened its doors, the Ohio Reform Farm and School was already experiencing the problems of overcrowding, with 58–65 boys per cottage. This complaint was echoed in 1876, 1893, 1903, 1929, and so on, as the population fluctuated due to economic factors such as wars and the Depression. Eventually a movement arose to close all institutions larger than 150–200 beds. (BIS/FSB.)

Six

TIME AND CHANGE ON THE HILL

All institutions change and evolve, even the most rigid and inflexible—even prisons. Sometimes it is by design, often by happenstance. The change might be abrupt and heralded or it might be imperceptible, recognized only in hindsight. It may only be a one-time response to a particular situation. Institutions are nothing if not laboratories for social experimentation. Consequently one person's experience can be markedly different than another's, yet both are "true."

The evolving nature of the Ohio Reform Farm and School is reflected in the various name changes that were enacted over its history. Each was prompted by a corresponding revision in the "science" of corrections. The original name was intended to convey the idea that the youth would be taught the virtues of hard work and a good education. In the early years, several names were used more or less interchangeably, such as Ohio Reform Farm School, Ohio Reform Farm, and Ohio Reform School.

In 1885, the facility was officially renamed the Boys' Industrial School. The reasons for this were, first, because it was never much of a farm to begin with owing to the poor soil; second, the boys were increasingly being trained to do industrial or factory-type work; and third, it was hoped to eliminate any stigma which might follow a boy as a result of having been a resident of a "reform school."

But as Shakespeare observed, "What's in a name?" The sign might have read Boys' Industrial School, but to most people it was still a reform school—a prison for juveniles. In 1964, the name was changed once more, this time to the more euphemistic Fairfield School for Boys. Obviously the desire was to escape the stigma that was now attached to the term "industrial school" by concealing the correctional institution behind a prep-school-like name. However, it also signaled a move away from trades and towards academics.

Of course, institutions change and evolve in other ways as well. For example, the original philosophy was to clothe the boys in military-style uniforms to set them apart from their peers. However, by the time the facility closed, the policy was to dress the boys in clothing that was not radically different from what they might wear back home (jeans and T-shirts, for example).

As a result, nothing that is said about these institutions held true throughout their history—only for a particular point in time and that time has passed.

Every morning, the boys assembled in Jennings Hall, received their instructions for the day, and then went off to their assignments. However, one company would remain behind to drill for two hours. Wearing military-style uniforms, the boys were expected to march whenever they moved as a group across the campus, whether to the dinner, school, vocational shops, and so on. In 1907, the U.S. Army issued the drill team 800 Springfield rifles. (BIS/FSB.)

As early as 1862, a band had been organized with instruments provided by the staff. In 1876, the school formed a brass band under the direction of Prof. J. C. Smith, the elder brother of the Maumee family. It originally included 10 boys, but by 1901 could boast 42 members and its own cottage, Lagonda. The 1928 band (with over 70 members) was considered the best in the institution's history. (BIS/FSB.)

In 1907, Dr. E. J. Emerick, superintendent of the Ohio Institution of Feeble-Minded, noted that examinations of 100 consecutive admissions to the Boys' Industrial School showed 46 were feeble-minded, 26 were borderline, 11 were mentally retarded, and only 17 were of normal intelligence. At the Girls' Industrial School, the results were even more discouraging: 56 feeble-minded, 14 borderline, 13 mentally retarded, and only 14 normal. (CCCJ.)

In 1887, an ice pond was constructed by the boys to supply ice for refrigeration. It later was expanded to create Reams Lake, named for public welfare director Harry Frazier Reams Jr. (who had prosecuted Thomas "Yonnie" Licavoli). The lily pond below the superintendent's house dates from 1901. It was necessary to dredge the pond periodically and clear it of excess vegetation to keep it picturesque. (BIS/FSB.)

Commissioner B. W. Chidlaw noted: "When a boy . . . swings the ax, handles the hoe, or holds the plow with a willing mind and a cheerful heart, we [know he will] be all right—self-reliant, able and willing to work; he will eat honest bread; and in his relations to society he will be a producer and not a consumer, a busy bee and not a worthless drone." (BIS/FSB.)

To "save" the boys, the Ohio Reform Farm employed a four-pronged approach to treatment: social, moral, intellectual, and industrial (or home, religion, school, and work). Many of the boys were orphans, or at least neglected, spent their time running the streets and had only a fleeting acquaintance with school and church. Any jobs they worked were apt to be illegal. This was the blacksmith shop, built in 1886. (BIS/FSB.)

In 1905, the Boy's Industrial School housed 920 offenders, ages 10 to 21, organized into a regiment with three battalions. The primary trades at that time were blacksmithing, floriculture, tailoring, baking, printing, carpentering, telegraphy, stenography, brick making, shoemaking, dairying, and cooking. They also operated the steam, cold storage, and electric plants, the barn, laundry, and poultry plant. This was the bakery. (BIS/FSB.)

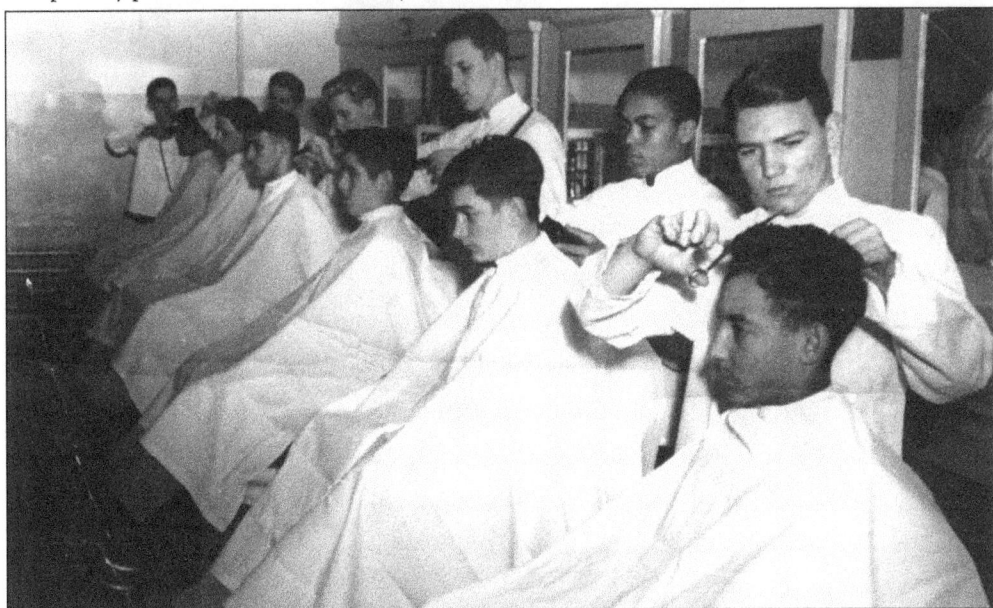

Until 1907, a family officer was responsible for cutting each boy's hair. However, it was decided to offer barbering as a shop class. In order to complete the program, it was often necessary for a youth to agree to remain at the Boys' Industrial School for several months following his official release date. After Boys' Industrial School closed, the program was moved to the Training Institution of Central Ohio in Columbus. (BIS/FSB.)

Hope, Lester.		20546	*Hocking*	Cleveland, O.	Cuyahoga.
Name		Number	Family	City	County

Received **May 18, 1918.**   Offense **J. D. P.**   Color **White,**

Where Born **England,**   Date **5/29/1903** Age **14** Court **Juv.**

Parentage **English.**   Residence **Cleveland, O.**

Education **8th.**   Truant **yes.**   Occupation **None,**   Religion **Presbyterian**

Heighth **5'**   Weight **105**   Hair **Brown,** Eyes **Brown,** Complexion **Fair,**

Tobacco **No.**   Intoxicants **No.** Profane **Yes,**   Language **Eng.**

Father Living **Yes,**   Mother Living **Yes** Stepfather   Stepmother

Parents Separated **No.**   Divorced   Lives With **Parents,**

Parents' Occupation **Stone Cutter,**   Brothers **6**   Sisters

Parents' Habits **Fair,**   Identification Marks

Lesley (misspelled here as Lester) Townsend Hope was twice committed to the Boys' Industrial School as a youth and ran away from the facility after the second time. Once he achieved fame as comedian Bob Hope, Gov. James A. Rhodes had his records sealed to spare him any embarrassment. However, Hope is said to have later donated sizable sums of money to the institution, although he never returned for a visit. (WF.)

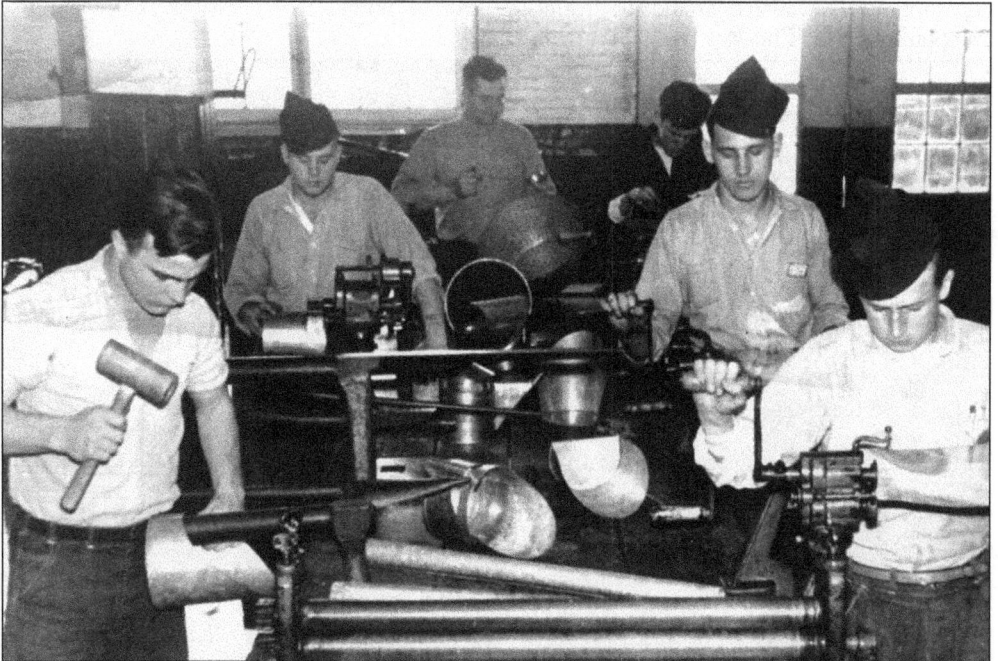

In this 1949 photograph, the boys are shown fabricating maple sugar water cans in the Tin Shop. These cans were used to tap the sugar maple trees, which grew in abundance in the Hocking Hills. The boys also manufactured the tin cans used in the institution's canning operation. Over time, a conscious decision was made to focus more on industrial trades and less on farming and horticulture. (BIS/FSB.)

Over the years, excess peaches, apples, grapes, strawberries, and various vegetables grown by the boys were processed, canned, and shipped to other state institutions. This helped to offset the cost of feeding the inmates at these facilities, reducing the tax burden on the public. However, some politicians argued that there was nothing rehabilitative about having an inmate work on a farm. (BIS/FSB.)

At 6:00 a.m., the boys ate breakfast in a common dining room, followed by devotional exercises and prayer. Then they moved in formation to the lawn where they were given the morning schedule. The schoolboys were dismissed first, then the shop, house, and team boys. Last, those who worked in the fields, gardens, or orchards, would go to the tool house to obtain the implements they needed for their duties. (BIS/FSB.)

At 11:00 a.m., the schools were dismissed, and the boys returned to the family buildings to clean up and relax before lunch. After dining, they would rest for an hour before lining up on the lawn once more. The boys that worked in the morning would now go to school and vice versa. At 5:00 p.m., it was time for a period of recreation and supper. (CCCJ.)

In the evening, each family met in their own schoolroom. The first hour was devoted to a review of each boy's conduct for the day. Then until bedtime at 9:00 p.m., the boys were to converse, read, sing, and amuse themselves however they liked in a quiet way—even blowing bubbles. Before retiring for the night, each boy knelt and spent a few moments in silent prayer. (BIS/FSB.)

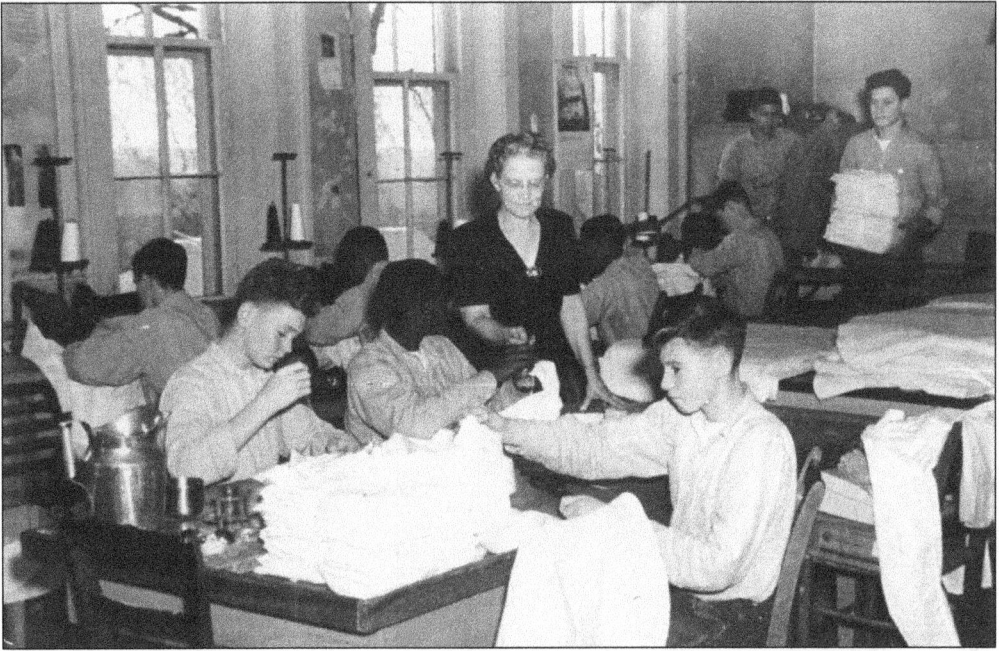

From the beginning, the tailor, carpenter, shoe, and blacksmith shops were intended solely to meet the needs of the institution. The officers of the reform school were always searching for opportunities to introduce new forms of industry that would provide the boys with meaningful and lucrative employment. For example, in 1867, they believed that the manufacturing of willowware would do just that, but they were limited by space. (BIS/FSB.)

Commissioner B. W. Chidlaw wrote in 1871 that although the lands were not well-adapted for agricultural purposes, he felt that their isolation, healthfulness, and suitability for "gardens, orchards, strawberry plantations, and vineyards" compensated for their unsuitability as farmlands. In truth, Charles Reemelin was more interested in viniculture than growing corn, wheat, or similar crops. Here the boys are picking (and eating) strawberries. (BIS/FSB.)

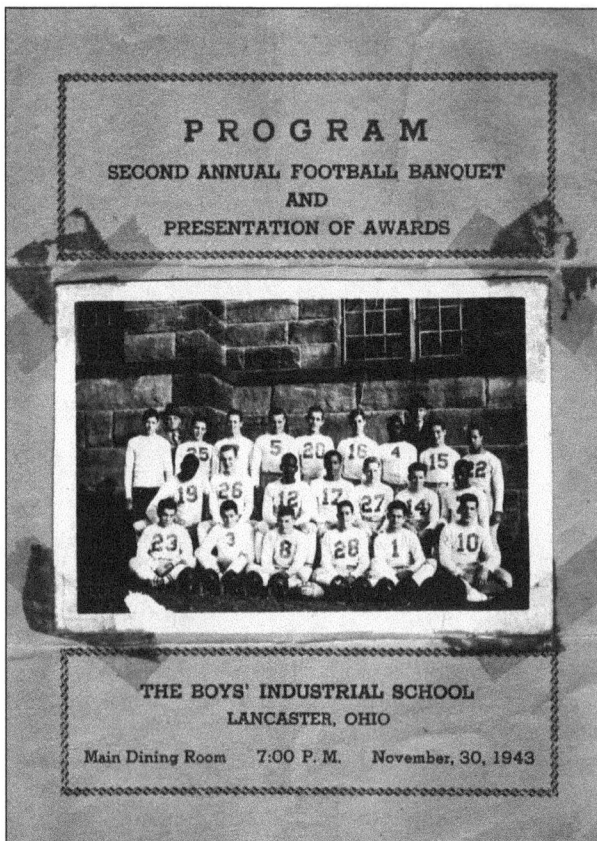

In 1943, G. S. "Kip" Owen and his assistant A. C. "Bennie" Berens coached the football team, taking them to games throughout the state. People were amazed at how well behaved the players were. A later coach even gave the team his watch and allowed them to get off the bus to walk for 15 minutes unsupervised on a Cleveland street. All were back on the bus before time had expired. (BIS/FSB.)

In the electrical shop, the boys learned how to wire circuits and perform small appliance repair. They also assisted with the electric generating plant that supplied the institution's power. One field in which Boys' Industrial School students especially excelled was telegraphy, and graduates for the program were quickly hired by the railroad, Western Union, and other employers throughout the state. (BIS/FSB.)

Each cottage operated as a "family"—not just any family, but "an intelligent, well-regulated, Christian home." The boys were taught "obedience and duty bring a sure reward, and that transgression has its inevitable penalty." For many, the institution was a better home than any they had ever known and they truly came to regard the staff and other youth as family. They even had a Boy Scout troop. (BIS/FSB.)

One youth wrote about the shoe shop for the *Boys' Industrial School Journal*, the institutional newspaper. He noted that they made new shoes and repaired worn ones, and added that Mr. Moore, their instructor, was "the coolest, mildest office[r] to work for; just ask the boys up here and they will flood you over telling you the nice things he does for us." (CCCJ.)

Another reporter for the newspaper wrote about the activities in the carpentry shop. At the time, there were a dozen boys assigned to it, busy working at the power plant and also tearing down the old greenhouse. Another group was occupied with repairing crates. He concluded his article with their motto, "A good promise is poor pay if not kept." (CCCJ.)

As early as 1871, the treatment system called for healthy competition among cottages, whether it was in sports, academics, drill, or simply keeping each cottage neat and orderly. Thus the boys were encouraged to support one another in positive behaviors and to place a check on negative behaviors, much as the members of an ideal family would. A century later, "Positive Peer Culture" was still being promoted. (BIS/FSB.)

William (Bill) Willis was among the first to "break" the color barrier in professional football when he joined the Cleveland Browns in 1946, a full year before Jackie Robinson did the same for major league baseball. In 1963, Willis was appointed director of the newly created Ohio Youth Commission by Gov. James A. Rhodes. It was felt he would provide the youth with a positive role model. (BIS/FSB.)

In the 1960s, several staff put together a "Festival of Lights" display that attracted hundreds of sightseers from the surrounding community. Visitors were also serenaded with Christmas carols by the institution's choir. Some 60 miles to the northwest, the Girls' Industrial School/Scioto Village had a similar event. Later superintendents had the displays at both institutions burned. (BIS/FSB.)

Owing to the success of the Ohio Reform School, a reform and industrial school for girls was authorized by the Ohio General Assembly on May 5, 1869. Modeled after the boys' institution, the State Reform School for Girls or Girls' Industrial Home was established on the west side of the Scioto River in Delaware County. It occupied the former White Sulfur Springs, a resort that dated back to 1847. (CCCJ)

In the gymnasium, the boys played games, staged concerts, listened to lectures, held dances, and acted in shows. In this particular production, they were joined by their counterparts at the Girls' Industrial School. When the two institutions staged the musical "South Pacific," the girls were bused more than 60 miles each way for daily rehearsals. For the monthly dances (with flowers donated by local funeral homes), they alternated institutions. (BIS/FSB.)

Seven

Souvenir of the Ohio
State Reformatory

Allen O. Myers was a true Horatio Alger hero. As a youth, he had been sentenced to the Ohio Reform Farm. However, he soon rose above his circumstances to become a newspaper reporter and Democratic member of the Ohio House of Representatives. Myers was something of a loose cannon, given to inflamatory rhetoric, political grandstanding, and stepping on the toes of friends and foes alike (he wrote the book *Bosses and Boodle in Ohio Politics*).

However, Myers was also an idea-man, and one of his best ideas culminated in the Ohio General Assembly's passing a series of laws, which in one fell swoop eliminated the contract system of employment, authorized indeterminate sentencing, created a parole system, mandated cumulative sentences for habitual criminals, and called for the construction of an "Intermediate Penitentiary."

In place of the contract system, the Ohio General Assembly had intended that prisoners work on so-called "State accounts." But having failed to appropriate the necessary funds to do so, the legislature passed a separate act permitting inmates to be employed on "the piece-price plan." Businesses were invited to provide machinery and materials so that prison labor could manufacture goods which the business could then purchase by the piece. The difference was the inmate no longer worked for the private employer, but for the state that had direct control over his working conditions.

The concept of indeterminate sentencing enabled the board of managers to decide the length of a sentence for a crime as long as it fell within the minimum and maximum limits as prescribed by law. In other words, an inmate could be released on parole (literally, his "word") if his behavior merited it. The first experiment with indeterminate sentencing had taken place at Elmira Reformatory in 1877.

As Superintendent James A. Leonard later wrote, "For centuries the most common method employed to protect society was imprisonment in a general place of confinement, into which all the weak, wicked, or broken offenders were cast without reference to age or character of the offense committed . . . based on the belief, 'once a criminal, always a criminal,' and with little thought as to methods of treatment calculated to improve character. These great prisons necessarily became schools of vice, from which men and women, with less of conscience but more of cunning, went forth to prey again upon society."

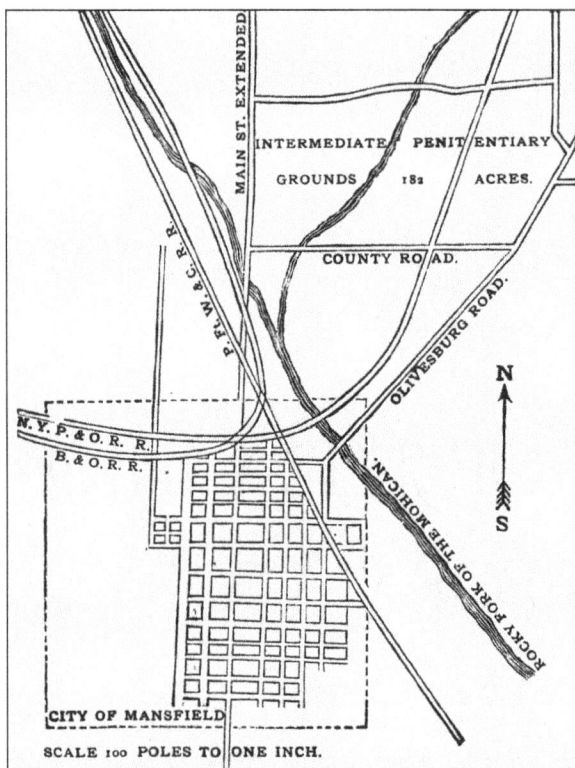

The Ohio legislature had authorized the construction of an intermediate penitentiary by an act passed on April 14, 1884. A year later, a board of managers appointed by Gov. George Hoadly selected Mansfield as the site of the proposed reformatory. With $10,000 contributed by the City of Mansfield and $20,000 by the state, they purchased the former Camp Mordecai Bartley, a Civil War training ground located a mile north of town. (Authors' collection.)

Although the cornerstone was laid on November 4, 1886 ("Mansfield's Greatest Day" proclaimed the headline in the *Richland Shield & Banner*), construction was not sufficiently advanced until September 18, 1896, to allow 150 short-term inmates to be transferred from the Ohio State Penitentiary. A day earlier, the name of the institution officially became the Ohio State Reformatory. (Authors' collection.)

In 1887, at the National Conference of Charities and Corrections in Omaha, celebrated social reformer F. B. Sanborn of Massachusetts had blessed the endeavor, declaring, "In Ohio, the board [of State Charities] has succeeded in establishing the most complete prison system, in theory, which exists in the United States. And this system is advancing toward practical development." (Authors' collection.)

Sprawling across the glaciated Richland County plain, the Ohio State Reformatory was one of the largest castle-like edifices in the country. But it was a castle with a difference, because instead of keeping people out, it was designed to keep them in (which it did rather successfully during its 94 years of operation). Its economic impact on the city of Mansfield was significant. (Authors' collection.)

Designed by Cleveland architect Levi T. Scofield (who also designed the insane asylums in Athens and Columbus), the reformatory was expected to cost $1.3 million. To help fund the project, the legislature earmarked 10 percent of the anticipated receipts from "the Scott law," a tax on the traffic in alcoholic beverages. However, the law was overturned by the U.S. Supreme Court the following year, curtailing one revenue stream and helping to delay construction for

a decade after the laying of the cornerstone. In fact, the reformatory still was far from finished when it opened in 1896. The first inmates, who had been cheered on by throngs of citizens in Columbus, Galion, and Mansfield, were put to work on the prison sewer system and built the 25-foot stone wall that surrounded the 15-acre complex. The east cellblock was not completed until 1908. (Authors' collection.)

This view of the prison yard dates to 1934, showing the smoke stack of the power plant and various shop buildings. In the 1989 movie, *Tango & Cash*, Kurt Russell and Sylvester Stallone escaped over the wall from the power plant roof. But, perhaps, the most memorable scene from the film was when Russell and Stallone walked through the cellblock while flaming litter rained down on them. (Authors' collection.)

As soon as the first inmates arrived by train from Columbus, they were marched directly to their cells in the western cellblock. "West Block" consisted of six tiers of cells with two ranges on each tier and 36 cells per range. There was one four-man cell and one one-man cell on each side of each range, while the rest were two-man cells for a total capacity of 876 men. (Authors' collection.)

"Three North" (actually 3 North East) was the protective custody range of the reformatory (approximately midway up in this photograph). Inmates housed here were regarded as likely targets for sexual and/or physical assaults or other types of exploitation. Some of them actually invited this sort of attention by wearing pool cue chalk for eye shadow, decorating their uniforms with pieces or ribbon, adopting feminine names, and the like. (CCCJ.)

Resembling nothing so much as a giant cage, the guardroom was the portal between freedom and captivity. The prison proper lay behind its iron-barred gate. On visiting day, inmates could receive members of their immediate families in this area. Even though the inmates were searched both before and after visitation, the guards had to be ever vigilant for items being smuggled in and out of the prison. (Authors' collection.)

Viewed from the air, the Ohio State Reformatory looked like a large factory but functioned more like a small town. Encompassed within a 15-acre plot of land framed by a 25-foot high wall were everything required for self-sufficiency, living quarters, dining hall, hospital, school, laundry, chapel, and various job assignments. Beyond the walls was a farm that provided much of the food consumed by the inmates. (CCCJ.)

Every prisoner admitted to the reformatory was fingerprinted and photographed, and a complete physical description which included age, height, weight, eye color, hair color, nationality/race, and any physical marks or tattoos was recorded on an identification card. Originally this was all handled by employees of the Identification Department. However, over time, inmate clerks performed many of these duties and became quite adept at classifying fingerprints. (Authors' collection.)

It has long been recognized that many inmates are poorly educated, and this may be a factor in their criminal behavior. Consequently the reformatory system emphasized correcting educational deficiencies when possible. It was not unusual for prisoners to complete high school and begin taking college classes during their confinement. Institutional schools are given innocuous names (such as Fields High School) so that a transcript does not stigmatize the student. (Authors' collection.)

Some inmates were assigned to manufacture clothing, including the "going home" suits issued to those being released. It was not difficult for those in law enforcement—and former inmates—to recognize these suits, so the newly released inmate was eager to exchange it for "civilian" clothes. However, some prisoners actually got to tailor their own suits and would endeavor to make them a little more stylish. (Authors' collection.)

It may be a cliché in Hollywood movies, but, in truth, many inmate plots and schemes are hatched in the prison laundry. The combination of noisy machines, humid working conditions, and inadequate supervision provides a good cover for whatever they might be planning. Baskets of laundry are ideal spots for hiding anything from a shiv to a fellow prisoner. (Authors' collection.)

One of the most volatile situations in any prison is mealtime. This arises from the fact that inmates take their food very seriously and have been known to riot when the quality or quantity does not meet their expectations. Furthermore the simple act of gathering hundreds of prisoners together at one time provides a forum for them to air their grievances and exact revenge upon one another. (Authors' collection.)

The officers had their own mess hall where they could order from a limited menu prepared and served by an inmate staff. In 1970, an ice tea was 15¢, a huge bowl of ice cream 10¢, and a T-bone steak 75¢. Unfortunately the fly problem was horrible and huge industrial fans were kept running in a vain attempt to keep the flies from settling any place for long. (CCCJ.)

Before much of the U.S. shoe industry moved overseas, shoemaking was actually a good trade for an inmate to learn. In the shoe factory at the Ohio State Reformatory, inmates turned out tens of thousands of shoes each year, which were worn by those in prisons, other state institutions, county homes, and children's homes throughout Ohio. They emphasized durability over style. (Authors' collection.)

Countless maple and oak desks, chairs, bookcases, and coat trees were turned out by the furniture factory at the Ohio State Reformatory. The craftsmanship was excellent and the prices were quite reasonable. However, there was a tendency for some inmates to use some of the finishes and solvents to get "high." Surprisingly there was little reluctance to put arsonists to work among the lumber and lacquers, despite the seeming temptations. (Authors' collection.)

Various state institutions, not just prisons, taught printing as a trade and successfully placed many of their graduates in well-paying jobs. At one time, the printing shop at the Ohio State Reformatory turned out most of the catalogs, annuals, and bulletins issued by state colleges and universities throughout Ohio, as well as various government publications. However, as technology changed, it became more difficult for them to keep up. (Authors' collection.)

This auditorium was actually the prison chapel, where weekly services were conducted for as many religious groups, denominations, and sects as there were in the inmate population. Chiefly these were Protestant, Catholic, Jewish, Christian Science, and, in later years, Muslim. Inmate boxing matches were staged here, as well as the "Little Show of the Big House," an inmate talent show which became something of a tradition. (Authors' collection.)

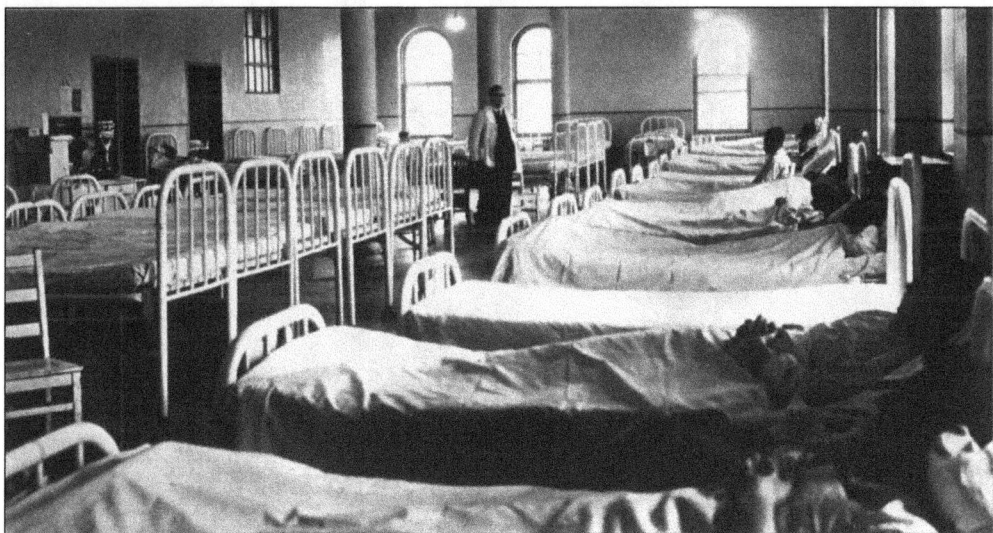

The prison hospital was set up to handle all but the most serious medical cases. Whenever several thousand people live together in close proximity, there is a real danger of communicable diseases spreading quickly if not properly diagnosed and treated. And some of the most desperate inmates will intentionally harm themselves in the hope that they will need to be transported to an outside hospital. (Authors' collection.)

The reformatory operated an excellent dairy herd, which supplied the institution with milk, cheese, butter, ice cream, and other dairy products. On a purely economic level, the use of inmate labor kept the cost of production extremely low. However, many would argue that the simple act of teaching the inmates how to be responsible for another living creature went a long way toward their rehabilitation. (Authors' collection.)

When the author joined it in 1970, the psychology department included (clockwise from bottom) Everett "Wes" Weston, Dave Hartman, Dave Randall, Don Randall, Jim Spindler, and Stu Van Dyke. They evaluated every inmate admitted to the institution and every inmate being considered for parole. They also had a say in all job assignments, discipline, and security classifications, while endeavoring to provide counseling to a caseload of several hundred apiece. (DR.)

106

Eight

DAYS AND NIGHTS IN DRACULA'S CASTLE

No one can say when the inmates began calling the Ohio State Reformatory "Dracula's Castle," but it probably was sometime after the 1931 release of the movie *Dracula*. Certainly, it is easy to imagine a black-caped Bela Lugosi stalking the shadows or vampire bats flitting about the towers. And since its closing in 1990, the surviving structure has gained a reputation as one of "The Scariest Places on Earth" thanks to cable television. In between, some unsettling things happened at the reformatory but not enough to satisfy modern day "ghost hunters" who have embellished the facts to suit their purposes.

To begin with, much of the stone for the reformatory was quarried locally, including from a site familiarly known as the Devil's Punch Bowl. Then, following her death on March 13, 1933, the ghost of the unfortunate eccentric Phoebe Wise has purportedly been seen walking along Reformatory Road. She had once been tortured by burglars who believed she was concealing a fortune in her tumbled-down house and later shot to death a madman who had been stalking her. However, purveyors of the paranormal have twisted the facts so that it is Wise who was murdered because it makes a better story.

During the Ohio State Reformatory's 94-year history, two guards or correctional officers were killed on duty, one at the West Gate and another in the vicinity of the "Hole." Not surprisingly, those investigators who have looked for it are convinced they have detected paranormal activity at both sites. They also claim to have seen the ghost of Helen Glattke, wife of a former superintendent, who died in an accidental shooting, as well as the ghost of her husband, Arthur, who suffered a fatal heart attack while in his office.

It is alleged on one Web site that "over 200 inmates died in this prison from fights and beatings," including one who made himself into a human torch and another who was killed by his cellmate when both were placed in solitary confinement together. The fact is over 135,000 inmates and thousands of staff passed through the reformatory, so it should come as no surprise that a few of them died, some by their own hand, some by natural causes, and a few through the actions of others. But, then, prison is a dangerous place because it is home to some dangerous people.

Until construction began on the Ohio State Reformatory, Mansfield's largest employer was Hautzenroeder and Company, a cigar manufacturer, with 285 employees. To the 15,000 or so citizens of Mansfield, the reformatory would come to represent a significant and dependable source of jobs. When it closed its doors in 1990, the city's population was just over 50,000. The reformatory was replaced by a smaller facility, the Mansfield Correctional Institution. (Authors' collection.)

When the influenza epidemic swept through the city of Mansfield, there was such a shortage of grave diggers that one father had to dig a grave for his own child. The mayor of Mansfield appealed to the reformatory for help, and scores of inmates volunteered. They were sent out in small work parties to dig graves in local cemeteries. The prison also has its own cemetery (shown above) where unclaimed bodies were buried. (CCCJ.)

In 1935, Arthur L. Glattke, appointed by Gov. Martin Davey to replace T. C. Jenkins as superintendent, moved his wife, Helen, and their children into the warden's suite at the reformatory. Ted, the younger son, has many fond memories of growing up at the institution, such as ice-skating on the pond. To the young boy, it seemed like "the largest inland body of water in the northern hemisphere." (Authors' collection.)

Tragically, on the morning of November 5, 1950, while preparing to attend mass, Helen (shown with her husband) accidentally knocked a loaded gun off a closet shelf. The gun discharged when it hit the floor, shooting her through the left lung. Helen called for her son Art Jr., who summoned his father, and she was rushed to a Mansfield General Hospital where she died two days later. (TG.)

A highly respected penologist, Arthur Glattke was well-liked by the guards and inmates alike, and is credited with instituting such reforms as the piping of music into the cells. In this photograph, the Glattkes are shown hosting a dinner party at the reformatory. Modern day ghost hunters have suggested that Arthur murdered his wife to avoid a divorce, but there is no evidence to support this. (TG.)

A. L. Glattke, Superintendent Of OSR, Dies; G. J. Allarding Is Acting Superintendent

Arthur L. Glattke, superintendent of the Ohio State Reformatory, died of a heart attack February 10.

Mr. Glattke was stricken in his office and died an hour later in the Mansfield General Hospital.

Named acting superintendent by M. C. Koblentz, chief of the Division of Correction, was George J. Allarding, OSR associate superintendent.

Mr. Glattke had been superintendent at Mansfield since 1935. From 1949 to 1954 he also served as acting chief of the newly-created Division of Correction.

A nationally prominent penologist, Mr. Glattke had served as president of the Wardens Association of America and of the Ohio Prison and Parole Association.

Prior to becoming superintendent at OSR, Mr. Glattke was a teacher and coach at Toledo Libbey High School and before that at Genoa High.

A native of Pittsburgh he was a graduate of Wittenberg College, where, in 1924, he was named All-Ohio Conference guard. He also took graduate work at Purdue University, the University of Michigan and the University of Toledo.

Mr. Glattke

Mr. Allarding

Arthur continued to serve as superintendent until he suffered a heart attack on February 10, 1959, while in his office. He did not die in the institution, however, as some ghost hunters have claimed, but was transported to Mansfield General Hospital where he passed away soon after arrival. As this obituary notes, he was acting chief of the newly created Division of Correction at the time of his death. (Authors' collection.)

George J. Allarding, named acting superintendent when Arthur died, was already residing on the second floor of the reformatory with his wife, while Dana M. Allen and his wife were on the third floor. Allarding and Allen were associate superintendents of the facility. A fourth family, that of Reverend Wapner, also occupied the second floor. Ted Glattke recalls that Reverend Wapner died in an automobile accident around 1961–1962. (Authors' collection.)

To the west of the Ohio State Reformatory was the prison honor farm, which stretched across to Route 13. On the edge of the farm were two houses owned by the reformatory, one occupied by Dr. John Horst, the institution's physician, and the other by John Niebel, the "Farm Superintendent." As Ted recalls, they used to refer to the reformatory as the "Farm" because of its positive atmosphere. (Authors' collection.)

John Elmer Niebel, his wife, Nolanda, and his 20-year old daughter, Phyllis, were part of the Ohio State Reformatory "extended family." As superintendent of the honor farm, John oversaw some 250 trustees who tended the dairy herd, the chickens and turkeys, the hogs, and the crops. An inmate had to prove himself at Niebel's honor farm before he could be transferred to a more distant one. (CCCJ.)

Early on July 20, 1948, Robert Daniels and John West, two recently paroled convicts, pulled their car up in front of the Niebel home. Bursting into the house while the family was still asleep, West pistol-whipped Niebel and his wife while Daniels beat and raped the daughter in another room. They had hoped Niebel could provide them with the address of a guard they harbored a grudge against. (CCCJ.)

Failing to get the information they wanted, Daniels and West forced the Niebels to strip, and then marched them into a nearby cornfield where they shot them to death. When the bodies were discovered a short time later, the alarm went out and what may have been the largest manhunt in Ohio history was put into motion. Newspapers quickly branded Daniels and West the "Mad Dog Killers." (CCCJ.)

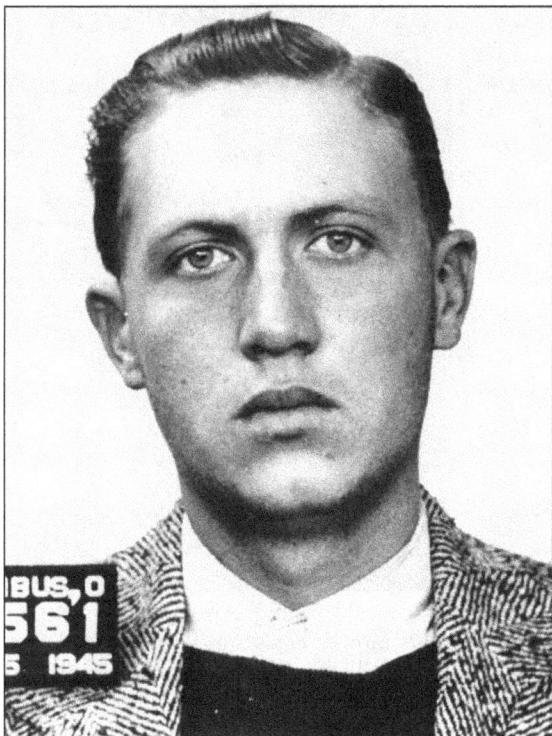

Daniels (shown in a 1945 mug shot) was described by a prison psychiatrist as "brainy," while West was viewed as mentally deficient. Although Daniels was the dominant personality, their "plan" was not well thought out. The duo made little effort to conceal their identities, driving Daniels's car, failing to wear masks, parking in front of the Niebel home, and so on. (CCCJ.)

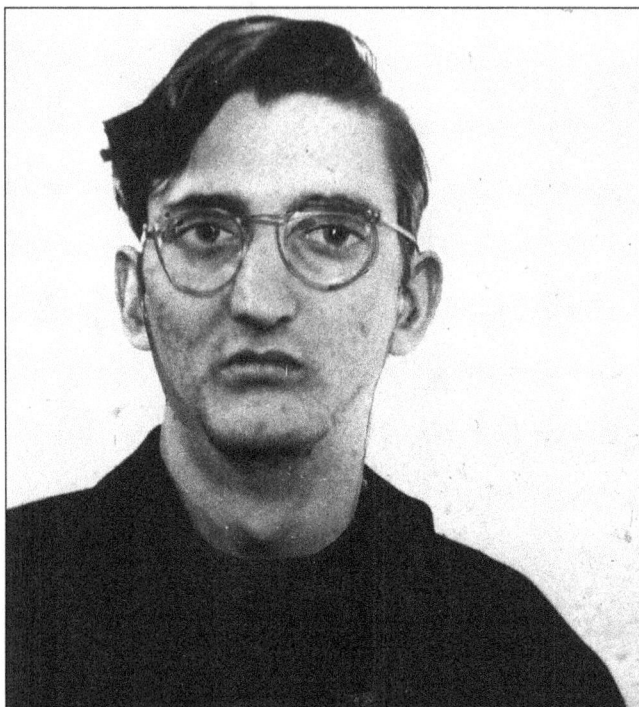

John Coulter West (shown in a 1948 mug shot) was thought to be generally harmless. He was befriended by Robert Daniels while they were both confined at the reformatory, and they made a pact to kill any guards who mistreated them. Released for "good behavior," the two began robbing taverns in Columbus. During their second robbery on July 10, 1948, they killed tavern owner Earl Ambrose. (CCCJ.)

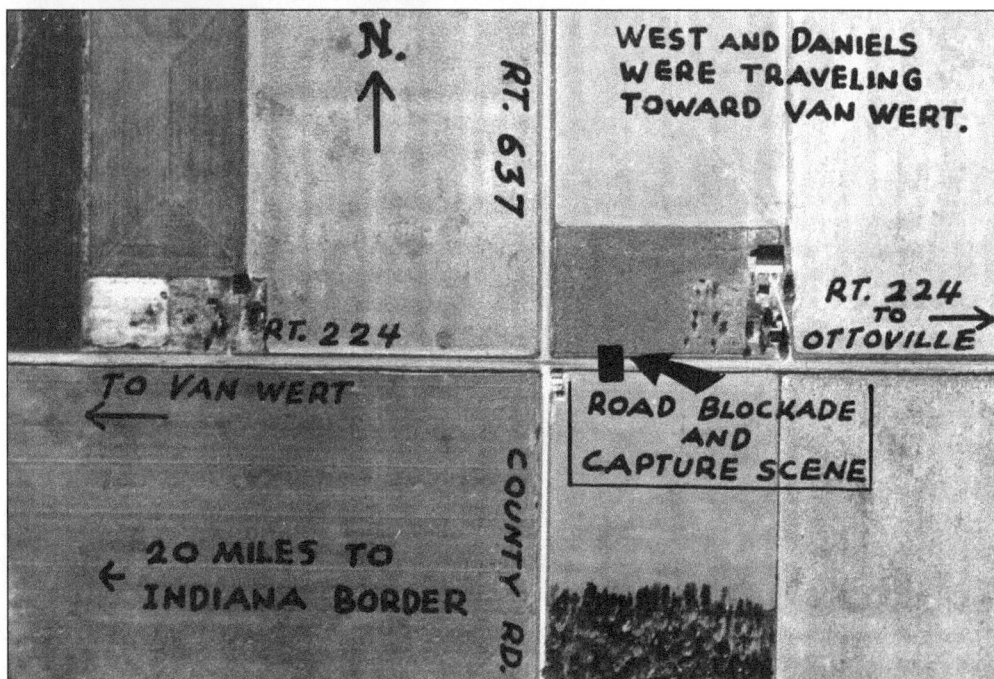

Fleeing the Niebel home, West and Daniels headed first for Cleveland. After attending a play and having dinner near Tiffin, they killed Seneca County farmer James Smith and stole his car. Smith's new bride escaped unharmed. They then killed Orville Taylor while he was sleeping in his truck and took his vehicle. Their murder spree came to an end at a roadblock in Van Wert County. (CCCJ.)

In a shootout at a police roadblock between Ottoville and Van Wert, West was killed, a police officer was injured, and Daniels meekly surrendered. While West's body was shipped to West Virginia for burial, Daniels stood trial for the Niebel murders in Mansfield. Found guilty in rather short order, he died in the electric chair on January 3, 1949. He was 24. (CCCJ.)

On November 3, 1926, while working the West Gate, 72-year-old guard Urban Wilford struggled with a former inmate who had returned to the reformatory in an effort to help a prisoner escape. Wilford was shot to death with a .38 caliber pistol. Two months later, Philip Orleck was arrested, tried, and sentenced to death in the electric chair. The execution was carried out the following year. (CCCJ.)

During an escape attempt on October 2, 1932, guard Frank Hanger, 48, was beaten to death with an iron bar. Inmates Merrill Chandler and Chester Probaski were subsequently found guilty of Hanger's murder and died in the electric chair on November 24, 1933. Guards or correctional officers (as they are now called) have difficult jobs but have been demeaned by most Hollywood films. (CCCJ.)

At the northwest corner of the reformatory was the Railroad Gate. Train cars could be switched into the prison yard for loading or unloading shipments. This was where the coal was brought into the institution for the power plant. In the 1976 movie *Harry and Walter Go to New York*, starring Elliot Gould and James Caan, this gate was "blown up" through Hollywood magic. (Authors' collection.)

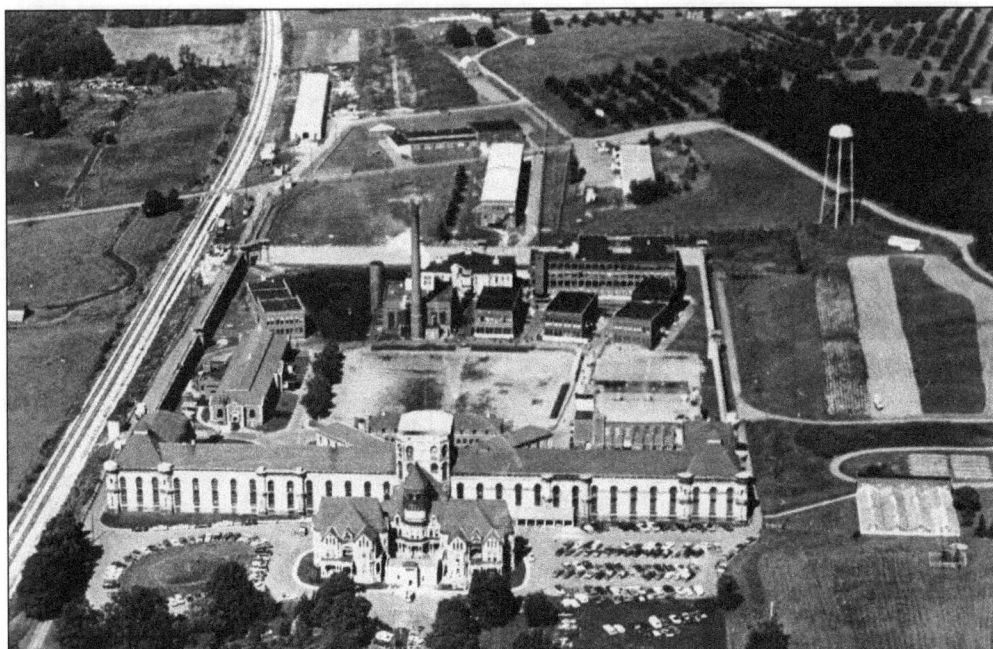

Construction started on the Ohio State Reformatory in 1886 and continued for nearly 75 years. As a result, it included a hodge-podge of architectural styles. When Hollywood began using it as a movie location, they had to deal with these visual anachronisms. Although *The Shawshank Redemption* was filmed in 1993, it was set in the 1940s. Consequently they had to avoid showing the newer dining hall and high school. (CCCJ.)

Some inmates who were deemed to be non-aggressive were sent to the Junction City Treatment Center, a former brick plant, to help them their overcome substance abuse problems. In the 1980 movie *Brubaker*, starring Robert Redford, Yaphet Kotto, and Jane Alexander, the facility substituted for the notorious Arkansas State Penitentiary, which was renamed Wakefield for the film. Redford's character was based on the true story of Thomas O. Murton. (CCCJ.)

Inmates who were judged by prison psychologists to be mentally ill were transferred to the Lima State Hospital for further evaluation and, it was hoped, treatment. When it came time to make a television movie, *Attica*, about the 1971 uprising at New York's Attica Correctional Facility, the filmmakers were denied access to the real prison, so they used Lima, even though it was still in operation. (CCCJ.)

Not all inmates lived within the reformatory walls. The farm dormitory, located between the prison and the barns, was home to 250 trustees whose work assignments involved the dairy barn, poultry farm, and the hoggery. Although there was always a risk in making an inmate a trustee, the fact is that all inmates at the reformatory were eventually going to be released anyway, whether or not they deserved it. (CCCJ.)

In September 1916, 20 years after the Ohio State Reformatory opened, 34 female inmates were transferred from the Ohio Penitentiary to the new Ohio Reformatory for Women in Marysville. It has grown into a multi-security facility with more than 2,000 inmates. At one time, it was a functioning farm with dairy cattle, hogs, and crops, and is still sometimes called the "Farm." (CCCJ.)

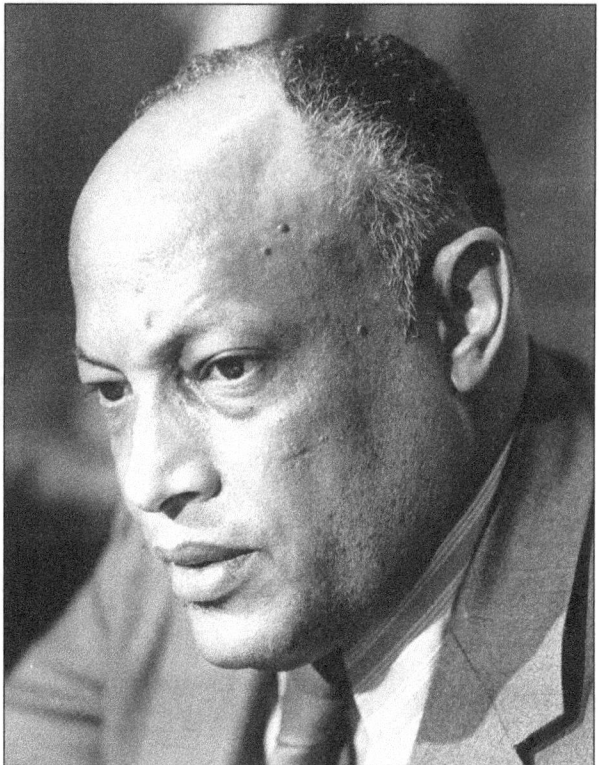

On August 28, 1970, Bennett J. Cooper, former superintendent of the Ohio State Reformatory, was named commissioner of the Ohio Division of Correction. Two years later, he became the first African American director of a Department of Corrections in the United States when the division broke away from the Department of Mental Hygiene and Correction. Cooper was also a founder of the National Association of Blacks in Criminal Justice. (CCCJ.)

In the 1997 Harrison Ford movie *Air Force One*, the Ohio State Reformatory was "cast" as the Russian prison in which Gen. Ivan Radek (played by Jurgen Prochnow) was confined. In this photograph, large paintings of Lenin and Stalin, left behind by the filmmakers, still loom over the guardroom. The reactivation of the Ohio Film Commission should help to bring more movie making to the Buckeye State. (MRCCVB.)

The Mansfield Reformatory Preservation Society is dedicated to maintaining, restoring, preserving, and showcasing the institution to highlight criminal justice in Ohio. Toward that end, they are actively raising funds to support their efforts and have rehabilitated the warden's living quarters, which can be rented for special occasions. (MRCCVB.)

Nine

HORROR AND SHAME OF CAMP CHASE

Camp Chase Military Prison is a sidebar to the history of corrections in Ohio. Located four miles west of Columbus on the National Road, Camp Chase was established in May 1861 as a training center for Union soldiers during the Civil War. It was named after former Gov. Salmon P. Chase and replaced the smaller Camp Jackson.

The first 23 prisoners arrived on July 5, 1861, but were permitted to return home to Virginia after a few days. Others soon followed, however, and with the fall of Fort Donelson in February 1862, a large contingent of Confederate officers were dispatched to Camp Chase on their word of honor (parole). Within a few months, more than a thousand prisoners were amassed—officers, enlisted men, and, in one instance, an officer's wife who refused to be left behind.

Gov. David Tod, self-proclaimed commander-in-chief, put minister Granville Moody in charge of the prison. In addition to personally conducting prayer meetings and sightseeing tours, Moody allowed Confederate officers to leave the prison and mingle with the citizens of Columbus. They strutted about the streets in full uniform, wearing sidearms, attended by their slaves who had accompanied them from Tennessee. Some booked hotel rooms, ate at local restaurants, and toasted the Confederacy in the city's saloons. A few even attended sessions of the state legislature.

Eventually complaints about lax discipline and poor management at Camp Chase led to an investigation. Not surprisingly, Moody was found to have "scant acquaintance" with military practices and procedures. Soon the federal government took control, increasing security, eliminating visitors, and censoring the mail. When another prison opened on Johnson's Island in Lake Erie, most of the officers were transferred there.

As the war continued, conditions at Camp Chase eroded further. Basic sanitation was lacking. The prisoners wore rags. The food was unhealthy. Facilities intended for 4,000 men were forced to accommodate nearly 7,000. Prison laborers built new barracks and sturdier fences, but the population continued to swell to 9,146 at its peak.

Of the estimated 25,000 Confederate troops who passed through Camp Chase, roughly 10 percent died while imprisoned. Then four years after the camp opened, the war ended with the surrender of Gen. Robert E. Lee and Gen. Joseph Johnston during April 1865. By July 5, all the remaining prisoners at Camp Chase were released, and within 18 months, the prison was dismantled, leaving only a cemetery.

This sketch was made from what was once the only known photograph of Camp Chase. Conditions within the prison were harsh. Food supplies were inadequate, diseases were rife, and mortality was high. Originally, deceased prisoners were buried in a city cemetery near present day Children's Hospital, but when Camp Chase established its own burial ground in 1863, 99 bodies were disinterred and moved to the new location. (CML.)

In recent years, historians Robert McCormick and David Roth identified four images in the National Archives taken by local photographer Manfred Griswold. The prison occupied an area 700 feet long by 300 feet wide boxed in by a 12-foot wooden fence patrolled by guards on a catwalk. A dozen or more prisoners occupied each of the 16-by-20-foot wooden shanties, surrounded by a sea of mud and filth. (NA.)

Camp Chase originally consisted of two prisons, side-by-side (a third was added later). Prisoners who took an oath of allegiance to the United States were housed in prison No. 2 where conditions were slightly better. These prisoners were called "Razorbacks" by those in prison No 1. In the barracks, prisoners slept in narrow bunks stacked three high, two men to a bunk, to keep each other warm. (NA.)

While in the military, Andrew Johnson, Rutherford B. Hayes, James Garfield, and William McKinley, were at Camp Chase, as well as Gen. Lew Wallace, who would author the best-selling novel *Ben Hur*, and Gen. John C. Freemont. It also held some of Morgan's Raiders, including Col. Basil W. Duke, and, until their discovery, a few "nymphs du pave" (prostitutes) who were disguised as men. (NA.)

Catherine Pemberton's house at 57 South Hague Avenue was one of the last surviving cottages that had been moved from Camp Chase when it closed. Camp Chase had been partially assembled from the remnants of Camp Jackson, which was located near present-day Goodale Park. When Camp Chase closed, most of the buildings were moved or dismantled. This photograph dates from 1898. (CML.)

A former Union officer, William H. Knauss, took an interest in marking the graves of Confederate soldiers who had died at the battle of Antietam. Through his efforts, annual memorial services were held at Camp Chase Cemetery beginning in 1896. It is estimated that more than 4,000 people attended the services in 1898. However, Knauss was not without his critics. (CML.)

With Gov. George Nash in attendance, a granite arch supporting a bronze statue of a Confederate soldier (facing south) was unveiled on June 7, 1902. Underneath was a huge boulder bearing the inscription "2260 Confederate Soldiers of the War 1861–1865 Buried in this Enclosure," although some of the remains have since been relocated. In 1906, Congress authorized the placement of white marble headstones on all the graves. (CCCJ.)

Camp Chase Cemetery had a ghost, the "Lady in Gray," who purportedly walked among the graves, searching for her lost husband. Some say she wept over the grave of Benjamin F. Allen, a private in the 50th Tennessee Regiment, Company D. First observed just after the Civil War, she eventually stopped making appearances. However, some believe she now roams the grounds of Nationwide Children's Hospital, site of the earlier graveyard. (CCCJ.)

Louisiana Ransburgh from Missouri married a wealthy Ohio farmer, Joseph Briggs, in 1867, settling near Camp Chase Cemetery. A proud daughter of the south, Louisiana took it upon herself to decorate the neglected graves of the Confederate soldiers, wearing a veil on her evening walks through the cemetery to conceal her identity. She became known as the "Veiled Lady of Camp Chase." This photograph shows a more recent visitor. (CCCJ.)

Smallpox struck the camp during the winter of 1863–1864, resulting in the deaths of hundreds. On the night of November 24, 1864, someone stole the bodies of six Confederate soldiers from the Camp Chase Cemetery. Several men, including Dr. Joab R. Flowers, were apprehended, but the bodies were never recovered (it is believed they were sold to a Cleveland medical school). Unrepentant, Flowers was later elected to city council. (CCCJ.)

126

Bibliography

Chidlaw, B.W. *The Story of My Life*. Philadelphia: William H. Hirst, 1890.

Coffin, E. G. *Souvenir of the Ohio Penitentiary*. Columbus, Ohio: privately printed, 1899.

Finley, James B. *Memorials of Prison Life*. Cincinnati: L. Swormstedt and J.H. Power, 1857.

Fogle, H. M. *The Palace of Death or the Ohio Penitentiary Annex*. Columbus: privately printed, 1909.

Fornshell, Marvin E. *The Historical and Illustrated Ohio Penitentiary*. Columbus: privately printed, 1903.

Gall, Joe. "Death of a Legend: Book Closing on Another Chapter in Ohio History." *Motive* (November/December, 1971).

Jenkins, T.C. *The Ohio State Reformatory 1896–1934*. Mansfield, Ohio: privately printed, 1934.

Jennings, Al. *Through the Shadows With O. Henry*. New York: The H.K. Fly Company, 1921.

Knauss, William H. *The Story of Camp Chase*. Nashville: Publishing House of the Methodist Episcopal Church, 1906.

Lore, David. "Inside the Pen." *The Columbus Dispatch*, October 28, 1984.

Mathews, J.H. *Historical Reminiscences of the Ohio Penitentiary*. Columbus: Chas. M. Cott and Company, Book Printers, 1884.

McCormick, Robert W. "About Six Acres of Land." *Timeline* (September/October 1994): 34–43.

Morgan, Dan J. *Historical Lights and Shadows of the Ohio State Penitentiary*. Columbus: privately printed, 1893.

Victor, Sarah M. *The Life Story of Sarah M. Victor or Mrs. Victor's Life Story*. Cleveland: The Williams Publishing Co., 1887.

Visit us at
arcadiapublishing.com